Journey to My Destiny

The World Is Waiting For You . . .

Stacie Gaynor

Copyright © 2012 – Stacie Gaynor

All rights reserved. This book is protected by the copyright laws of the United States of America. This book may not be copied or reprinted for commercial gain or profit. No part of this book may be reproduced in any manner without the expressed consent of the publisher, except in cases of brief excerpts in critical reviews and articles. Unless otherwise identified, Scripture quotations are from the Holy Bible, King James Version. Scripture quotations marked NIV® are taken from the Holy Bible, New International Version®. Copyright © 1973, 1978, 1984 by International Bible Society. Used by permission of Zondervan. All rights reserved. Scripture quotations marked NLT, are taken from the Holy Bible, New Living Translation, copyright © 1996. Used by permission of Tyndale House Publishers, Inc., Wheaton, IL 60189 USA. All rights reserved. All emphasis within quotations is the author's addition. Please note that FYI Publishing's style capitalizes certain pronouns in Scripture that reference the Father, Son, and Holy Spirit. Take note that the name satan and related names are lowercased. We choose not to acknowledge him, even if it is a violation of grammatical rules.

Journey To My Destiny by Stacie Gaynor

ISBN-10: 0985386312
ISBN-13: 978-0-9853863-1-3

Printed in the United States of America

FYI Publishing
P.O. Box 941665
Houston, TX 77094

Additional copies of this book may be purchased at
www.journeytomydestiny.com

Dedication

To the memory of Theodore and Sammie Gaynor, my parents.

To the love and support of precious family, friends, mentors, teachers, faith partners, champions, heroes, and sister-friends.

To the futures of my nieces, nephews, and godchildren:
Brett, Cher, Veronique, Perry, Mykala,
Shantel, Courtnie, and Christian.

To all people, everywhere
who are searching for their 'why?'

To your glory, Lord.
Without you, the journey would be meaningless.

Contents

Foreword i
Introduction iii

Part I - Order My Steps

Chapter 1   The Purpose of the Journey 1
Chapter 2   Who Are You? 11
Chapter 3   Discovering Your Purpose 25
Chapter 4   Moving Toward Your Destiny 43

Part II - The Adventure

Chapter 5   Survivor: Ain't No Mountain 59
Chapter 6   Through The Valley 73
Chapter 7   Purpose In The Pain 87
Chapter 8   Changing Your Course – Growing into Greatness 95
Chapter 9   Who's In Your Life? 113
Chapter 10 Life is a Trip 129

Part III - Sacred Places

Chapter 11 Secrets of the Seasons 145
Chapter 12 Write the Vision 153
Chapter 13 Your Assignment 167
Chapter 14 Return to the Garden 181
Chapter 15 The Sacred Cave 197
Chapter 16 The Perfect Storm 211
Chapter 17 Water in the Desert 227

Part IV - Inherit the Earth

Chapter 18 Journey to the Palace 243
Chapter 19 ARISE – It's Your Time 263

About The Author 275

Foreword
By Dr. Myles Munroe

This erudite, eloquent, and immensely thought-provoking work gets to the heart of the deepest passions and aspirations of the human heart to discover a sense of Destiny and Purpose.

Journey to My Destiny is indispensable reading for anyone who wants to live life above the norm. This is a profound authoritative work which spans the wisdom of the ages and yet breaks new ground in its approach, and will possibly become a classic in this and the next generation.

This exceptional work by *Stacie Gaynor* is one of the most profound, practical, principle-centered approaches to this subject I have read in a long time. Her approach to this timely issue of Destiny and Purpose brings a fresh breath of air that captivates the heart, engages the mind and inspires the spirit of the reader.

The author's ability to leap over complicated theological and metaphysical jargon and reduce complex theories to simple practical principles that the least among us can understand is amazing. This work will challenge the intellectual while embracing the laymen as it dismantles the mysteries of the soul search of mankind and delivers the profound in simplicity.

Stacie Gaynor's approach awakens in the reader the untapped inhibiters that retard our personal development and her antidotes empower us to rise above these self-defeating, self-limiting factors to a life of exploits in spiritual and mental advancement. The author also integrates into each chapter the time-tested precepts giving each principle a practical application to life making the entire process people-friendly.

Every sentence of this book is pregnant with wisdom and I enjoyed the mind-expanding experience of this exciting book. I admonish you to plunge into this ocean of knowledge and watch your life change for the better.

> Dr. Myles Munroe
> BFM International
> ITWLA
> Nassau Bahamas

Introduction

There are no ruby slippers, no magic wand to whisk you away to your destiny. Life is a journey and we must take it one step at a time. But every journey has its own unique geography. Expect this book to take you through the discovery process as you learn the significance of the mountains, valleys, and storms in your life.

In *"Journey To My Destiny,"* you will not only understand the purpose of your journey but how to overcome every obstacle along your path. When you learn to navigate the geography of your life, you take dominion of your world!

Step by step, from chapter to chapter, as the journey unfolds you will not just read, but experience your very own journey of discovery. Chapter "Reflections" and personalized exercises are designed to move you from *inspiration* to *demonstration*. Be empowered to ascend from your valley and move mountains from your path. Experience the fascinating journey through *The Sacred Cave*, the adventure of the *Safari* where you will overcome your fears, and the serenity of *The Garden* where you will experience an unforgettable encounter. You will give birth to your visions and be refreshed by *Water in the Desert*. Above all, you simply cannot miss the spectacular *Journey to the Palace*, where you understand that you may not have chosen these times, but these times have chosen you!

Where are you in life? How did you get there? Where is the journey leading you?

Prepare to search the deepest places of your heart and soul and be genuinely inspired to awaken to your place of divine destiny. Forge ahead through tragedy and triumph and discover the truth of who you are, why you are here, and what you were "sent" to do. But be warned.

The journey could forever change your course in life! Are you ready to *become the person God created you to be?*
   Are you ready to take the journey?
   The world is waiting for you...

Part I
Order My Steps

Chapter 1
The Purpose of the Journey

Everyone is on a journey. Each human being has a set course in life with a path that intertwines and connects with the paths of others, forming what we call our "world." The pages ahead will take you over high mountains and through dark valleys, across vast seas and dry lands (i.e., the geography of life). But to what end? Are we endless wanderers until death, or is there purpose to our lives on earth?

Time and Eternity

First things first. News Flash: You existed in the mind of God before you were ever placed in the earthly realm. You didn't have a human body, but He knew you and chose you before the foundation of the world (Eph. 1:4). Consider that you were not just born into the earth, but "sent" for a specific purpose and to fulfill a divine mission here.

Can you imagine that? Decisions you make during your moments on earth (called "time") will determine the path you take and also will have eternal consequences.

> *"Your eyes saw my unformed body; all the days ordained for me were written in your book before one of them came to be."*
>
> (Ps. 139:16, NIV)

How awesome is it that God keeps a "baby book" for each of His children? In it, the plan He desired for your life was pre-written – day by day, step by baby step. In another scriptural example, Jeremiah was ordained to be a prophet before he was born:

> *"I knew you before I formed you in your mother's womb. Before you were born I set you apart and appointed you as my prophet to the nations."*
>
> (Jer. 1:5, NLT)

This verse is one example of how God imparted various gifts to each of us before we emerged from our mother's womb. "I knew you" is the same connotation as "Adam knew Eve, his wife" (Gen. 4:1). Just as Adam was intimate with Eve, knew her and deposited a part of himself into her, God knew you in the spirit and deposited something within you. The concept of being intimate with the almighty God seems irreverent to us, yet it is what He desires most.

> *"Now it is God who makes both us and you stand firm in Christ. He anointed us, set his seal of ownership on us, and put his Spirit in our hearts as a deposit, guaranteeing what is to come."*
>
> (2 Cor.1:21-22, NIV)

"I knew you," also means knowing all about you – your weaknesses, limitations, personality, mood swings, and imperfections. He knew it all, and still, He called you!

He knows each of us as if there were only one of us to know, and loves each of us as if there were only one of us to love, in spite of our shortcomings.

The womb is the backstage dressing room where you are being fitted for your earth suit. The curtains open on the day you are born, announced, and presented to the world. The stage is set for a grand performance. But from beginning to end, God knows all the scenes of your life. From Act I until the final scene, He knows. All the drama? He knows! Yet, He has great expectations of your performance.

> He knows each of us as if there were only one of us to know, and loves each of us as if there were only one of us to love

> *"For I know the thoughts that I think toward you, saith the LORD, thoughts of peace, and not of evil, to give you an expected end."*

(Jer. 29:11)

Your Divine Destiny

You are a work of art!

The almighty God breathed life into you. Contained in that breath of life were all the wonderful things that make you: your gifts, dreams, personality, and talents, neatly gift-wrapped by your body. He stored those things inside of you so that at the appointed time He could call forth those things to be used for His divine purpose and glory. That stirring within you to pursue greatness and excellence simply signifies that God is making a demand on His deposit.

Have mercy!

Can't quite see it? Well, as a single thread in the vast tapestry of humanity, it's difficult to see your distinct and unique purpose. Truthfully, you will never fully see it through natural eyes. But you can through God's eyes, the One who created this work of art called "you."

> *"The eyes of your understanding being enlightened; that you may know what is the hope of His calling, and what the riches of the glory of His inheritance in the saints,"*

(Eph. 1:18-19)

> The destiny you desire is hidden in God!

The destiny you desire is hidden in God! Through human eyes it may be distorted. Through the eyes of the enemy it is perverted. Through divine eyes it is perfect.

> *"For now we see through a glass, darkly; but then face to face: now I know in part; but then shall I know even as also I am known."*
>
> (1 Cor. 13:12)

How do we see things through God's eyes?

You must search the heart of God. Certain things will only come by revelation from Him. The chapter titled "The Garden" will explore seeking the heart of God.

> *"You will seek me and find me, when you seek me with all your heart."*
>
> (Jer. 29:13, NIV)

Some believers wonder: Is God really interested in whether or not I succeed?

> *"... Let the Lord be magnified, which has pleasure in the prosperity of His servant."*
>
> (Ps. 35:27)

So the answer is yes! He wants us to be productive or fruitful. He is the vine and we are His branches.

But I don't feel qualified, they argue.

> He anoints us to do what He appoints us to do.

Whom the Lord calls He equips. (See 1 John 2:27; Eph. 2:10.) He anoints us to do what He appoints us to do.

The beautiful thing about walking in divine destiny is that you are moving in His Spirit and His strength, not your own. All He requires of you is a willing heart and an obedient spirit. Through the wisdom of God, *you will do what you couldn't do before and know things you didn't know before.* He has promised to give you knowledge of witty inventions (Prov. 8:12). You will be amazed at the difference between what you can perform with your own abilities and the awesome thing God can do through you!

Within your destiny are many paths that you are pre-ordained to travel. Completion of a single path does not signal the completion of your total destiny. There's more! The fact that you can only see the path you are on in no wise means that's all there is. Your journey is a step by step process, line upon line, precept upon precept. But if you have a misstep in Act 1 Scene 1, the play is not over. If you didn't give your best performance in Scene 2, you get a chance to regroup and refresh yourself, and come back and give it all you've got in Scenes 3 and 4. Circumstances may demand that you fail, but you can rewrite the script by getting back on the same page as the plan God has for you.

Don't Miss the Moment

Something inside of you longs to actively seek the true meaning of your existence. Every person on earth has a moment in time when they pause and wonder, why am I really here? When that moment occurs, don't dismiss it, because you are standing at a crossroads that will change the very course of your life. Your positive reaction to that moment sets in motion God's pre-ordained destiny for your life. It is there that you decide to pursue true destiny or continue on the way of man. If you think you have missed that moment in your life, go back and get it! It is the most important day of your life.

My moment came as I faced a life and death situation. Yes, I chose death. But through a TV program, I received a timely message that inspired me to pursue purpose. Looking back, had Dr. Myles Munroe not been in position and on assignment to release across the airways the revelation God had given him about purpose, I might not have lived to tell share *Journey to my Destiny* today. You will read more about my experience in a later chapter, but right now, let's focus

> Someone else's destiny is dependent on whether or not you step into yours!

on you, because *someone else's destiny is dependent on whether or not you step into yours!*

Gift Wrap

Think of the most beautiful building you've ever seen. The Taj Mahal, for instance. Or the Great Pyramids of Egypt. They are some of the world's most impressive structures. Makes you wonder what's inside, doesn't it? Something important? Something mysterious?

I am often delighted by beautifully wrapped gifts. It hardly matters what's inside as long as I get a chance to "ooh and aah" at the packaging before it's opened. Sometimes I save the packaging like, forever. And when I give gifts in pretty bags, there's a subtle tug-of-war before I release it. Oh, you can keep the gift, but I want my beautiful bag back! Well, this is one of those instances where I'm glad to say that God's ways are not our ways. He is far more interested in the gift on the inside. The gift wrap will return to the dust, but the gift inside lasts forever.

Gift wrap is what you see when you look in the mirror, but God's desire is for what He placed on the inside to manifest so greatly that the outside packaging is hardly noticeable.

You should feel honored to have been chosen to house and protect such a precious gift. As a vessel of honor, you must respect the treasures within you and within others as your divine responsibility. Try not to judge others superficially and according to outward appearance of the container. Instead, behold the treasure within.

Picture how you typically unwrap a gift. Do you tear into it with excitement and anticipation? If so, the gift wrap can never be used again. Unwrapping the gift too soon spoils the moment. *There is an appointed time for the unveiling of your gift.* Premature exposure can render your gift ineffective. Don't allow man (no matter how well meaning) to pressure you and rip away at you in the excitement of seeing what's on the inside–seeing what you're made of. God knows how and when to release His gifts. He does not expose; He *reveals* and *unveils*, leaving what's inside of you intact. By revealing, you become more transparent and less noticeable as the gift inside increases.

As the Story Goes...

On the sixth day of creation a meeting took place in Heaven.

God gathered all the heavenly hosts together to decide where to hide the secret of life.

Michael, the archangel, boldly spoke first. "Bury it beneath a great mountain. Man will never find it there."

But the four and twenty elders said, "No, one day man will find the means to dig and excavate and discover the secret of life."

Four cherubim flew in together and in unison cried, "Hide it in the oceans deep. They'll never find it there."

But the seraphim responded, "No, someday humans will discover ways to travel deep into the oceans and will find the secret of life."

Just then, Gabriel sounded his golden trumpet and all Heaven was silent.

Then a nameless, faceless being stood and said, "Place it inside of them. They'll never think of searching there."

All of Heaven agreed. And God hid the secret of life within us.

God has hidden his greatest gold inside of you!

"But we have this treasure in earthen vessels, that the excellency of the power may be of God, and not of us."

(2 Cor. 4:7)

Just remember, whatever is hidden away in God is not hidden *from* you, but *for* you.

> Whatever is hidden away in God is not hidden from you, but for you.

Deep within you lies a destiny. It's worth your time to research it, until every cell, every fiber of your being cries, "This is what I was born for!" And your life will never be the same.

The Journey

There are no ruby slippers, no magic wand to whisk you away to your destiny. The journey is a process. If you trust the process, it will take you where you want to go. But it will change you. The purpose of the journey is not to arrive; the purpose of the journey is to "become." Like the butterfly, the beginning stages of your journey may not look very appealing, but in time you will emerge from the cocoon having your life transformed into something beautiful.

Can you imagine the fulfillment of becoming everything God made you to be? Everywhere you go, every life you touch with your glorious new existence will be because of your commitment and faithfulness to the journey.

Now that you've awakened to the possibilities, welcome to your life!

No longer should you be hidden and trapped in the dungeons of darkness. Pull back the drapes, throw open the windows, and take in the view. It won't all be easy, but it promises to be adventurous, colorful, and amazing. You will look back and say, there may have been simpler times, even easier times, but never more exciting times!

> The purpose of the journey is not to arrive; the purpose of the journey is to "become."

As you read on, expect this book to take you through the discovery process. Find the significance of the mountains, valleys, heartaches, and triumphs in your life. Discover your own personal journey. You will learn, you will grow, and you will be fulfilled.

You will find your personal pathway to purpose.

Prepare for your incredible journey!

Reflections Of The Journey

- You were not just born into the earth realm, but "sent" for a specific purpose.

- The destiny you desire is hidden in God!

- Whatever is hidden away in God is not hidden from you, but for you.

- God anoints you to do what He appoints you to do.

- Someone else's destiny is dependent on whether or not you step into yours!

- There is an appointed time for the unveiling of your gift.

- The purpose of the journey is not to arrive. The purpose of the journey is to "become."

The Journey Continues . . .

Chapter 2
Who Are You?

L et's first establish who you are not:
- You are not your weaknesses.
- You are not your mistakes.
- You are not your past failures.
- You are not your family's pattern of lack, abuse, or disease.

Knowing your true identity comes not by your own definition, but by seeing yourself through the eyes of He who made you. God's book is full of the thoughts, plans, and ideas He has about you and how you fit into His master plan. Every human being was designed with this in mind. *The journey into the wilderness is all about knowing Him, knowing who you are in Him, and trusting that He is fully able to bring you out of your present circumstances into your promised land.* Let's explore.

Wilderness Of Doubt

Satan challenges our destiny by causing us to question who we are. If he is successful here, we become drifters and wanderers, victims of our circumstances who are never able to fully realize our capabilities. It renders us impotent. What good is a king who doesn't know he's king?

You cannot hinder suggestions of doubt coming into your mind. You can, however, refuse them. They are not your doubts unless you accept and consent to them.

> Get into agreement with what God says about you.

How do you resist doubt? Get into agreement with what God says about you. You must know who you are. After Jesus was born, the Bible gives no account of satan confronting Him until the time came for the launch of His dynamic ministry. Then He had a major encounter and Jesus was tempted with doubt.

> *"Then was Jesus led up of the Spirit into the wilderness to be tempted of the devil. And when He had fasted forty days and forty nights, He was afterward an hungered. And when the tempter came to Him, he said, "If thou be the Son of God, command these stones be made bread." But He answered and said, "It is written, Man shall not live by bread alone, but by every word that proceedeth out of the mouth of God."*
>
> (Matt. 4:1-4)

Again and again the devil tempted Jesus, offering Him the kingdoms of the world if only He would worship him. Three words the devil used repeatedly were "If thou be." In other words, are you really who you say or think you are? But Jesus didn't doubt. He didn't even entertain the question. Every time the devil said "If thou be," Jesus countered with his own three words *"It is written!"* He knew the Word of God was the most powerful defense. And surely, the devil did flee.

This is our example. Whenever satan discounts our lives as invaluable and insignificant, we too must respond by saying *"It is written."* The Word of God is always our best defense.

> The wilderness of doubt is a test of your character and confidence.

As you embark upon your journey, it is certain that *the first enemy you will encounter is doubt and temptation.* Do you know what is written about you? It is vital that you know and hold on to the Word of God that declares who you are. Search the Scriptures and openly confess God's promises and declarations. As it was with Jesus, so shall it be with you. Know that when the devil begins to whisper words of doubt in your ear, you are on the brink of greatness, just as Jesus was!

The Exodus

The children of Israel were released from the bondage of Egypt with the anticipation and excitement of entering the Promised Land. This was their Exodus – *coming out of something to move into something greater.* However, they were greatly disappointed that their pathway to promise led them through the wilderness. Prepare for your Exodus, your coming out of something (negativity, poverty, obscurity, abuse, old habits, etc.) to move into your wealthy place. But to get there, you must go through the wilderness. How long you wander in the wilderness will be determined by your obedience, attitude, and decisions.

The wilderness of doubt is a test of your character and confidence. Surviving it determines whether you move to the next level in your destiny. There are just some things God won't place in your hands until He knows He can trust you. If you haven't successfully been tested, how certain is it that you can be trusted with His vision and plan? If you hold on to God's Word that declares you are who He says you are, and openly confess it, you will not only survive the wilderness of doubt and temptation, but come forth with power and step into the greatness God has ordained for you.

The Devil's Prayer

Imagine that every morning in hell the devil gathers all the demons together to start their day off in prayer. If the devil had one prayer, I think it would be very short and go something like this: "Please, oh please, oh please don't let the people of God discover who they really are! Amen." In other words, don't let parents know they have been empowered to pray over their children before they leave for school to protect them from sickness or harm. And don't let husbands and wives know that the marriage of two who become one is the most powerful agreement on earth. And don't let believers know there are a host of heavenly angels on assignment awaiting instruction to help them carry out their purposes. And don't let them know they have power to get wealth. And...

The Matrix

I have yet to see the movie *The Matrix* in its entirety. It seems I always tune in toward the end, the part where Morpheus believes Neo is "the one" sent to save them, but Neo has been led to believe there is nothing particularly special about him. Then, when it seems the enemy is overtaking him, Neo's genius starts to emerge. Morpheous says of Neo, *"He's beginning to believe."* In other words, he's starting to know who he is! Neo then rises up and whips the enemy with one hand behind his back. His feet are planted and he is barely exerting himself. Something about knowing who you are makes the task at hand seem almost effortless.

Like it or not, the film contains a hint of Christian doctrine—one man sent to free a people who believe in a place called Zion, and letting go of fear, doubt and disbelief to release your innate abilities. But the Matrix is imaginary, you say. Still, it has a meaningful and timely message. What is *not* imaginary is the reality of who you are:

It is written, you are:
- An eternal being, not a blip on the radar screen. (Eccl. 12:7)
- God's beloved creation, fearfully and wonderfully made. (Ps. 139:14)

- The only earthen vessel made to house the awesome glory of God. (1 Cor. 3:16)
- The one given dominion over every other living thing on earth. (Gen. 1:26)
- The apple of His eye. (Zech. 2:8)
- The only being made in God's image and as a speaking spirit. Gen. 1:26
- Empowered to multiply His Kingdom throughout the earth. (Gen. 1:28)
- So important that the angels are assigned to guard and keep you. (Ps. 91:11)
- So desired that God sent His only Son to redeem you from sin and restore you back to the Kingdom. (John 3:16)
- So beloved that God knows the very number of the hairs on your head. (Luke 12:7)
- So valuable that heaven wars against hell for your sake. (Isa. 59:19, Deut. 33:27)
- So interesting to God that He records everywhere you go in His book, and so precious He keeps your tears in a bottle. (Ps. 56:8)

Be sure to complete the "It Is Written (I Am) exercise at the end of the chapter.

As you boldly declare God's Word and come into agreement with what it says about you, you will have mixed reviews from the crowd. Your enemies will sneer and doubt. But heaven will smile and say, *"She's beginning to know who she is."*

But wait! There's more.

As a covenant believer, you are:
- The head, and not the tail. (Deut. 28:13)
- Above only, and not beneath. (Deut. 28:13)
- Blessed coming in and going out. (Deut. 28:6)
- Joint heirs to the throne of God with Christ Jesus. (Rom. 8:17)
- A citizen from Heaven, representing God's Kingdom on earth. (Phil. 3:20)

That's who you are!

Belonging

For the first few years of my life, I didn't know who I was or where I belonged, because I didn't know where I came from. As one of many practical jokes, my older siblings had convinced me that I was adopted, only they forgot to say "April fool!" I only half believed them at first, until one day we were looking through the family album at all of our baby pictures. There were several of my brother and sister, but none of me. As usual, I didn't ask why. I didn't want to spoil the fun. I just got quiet.

But from then on, I began to imagine the family I must have come from. Why didn't they keep me? What was wrong with me? I imagined stories of why they gave me away. Mostly, I dreamed of an imaginary older sister named Debbie. She was nice and very protective of me.

When I was nine years old, we moved into a new house. Mom was busy unpacking and sifting through a box in the back of a tall chest of drawers. She called to me from the bedroom, "Teenie, come see what I've found!"

It was my birth certificate. She was reading it to me and describing it, while I tugged fiercely at her pant leg. I wanted to see. She bent down and showed it to me. "See, there's your name."

I looked it over and pointed at the bottom. "And is that your name?"

She was still sorting through the other papers she had in her hand, "Oh look, Teenie, here's your feet!" Her dimples widened as she smiled. But it was those two little tiny inkblot footprints that made me water up. "What's the matter, honey?"

I had my hands behind my back, twisting the heels of my shoes over. Then I asked her, "So, you're my real mommy?"

"Well, of course I am. Why would you—"

"You mean ... I'm not adopted?"

"Adopted! What would make you think such a thing?"

When I told her the story my brother and sister had weaved, she laughed and laughed. Once she told me the truth, and showed me the truth (the third Cesarean scar on her belly), I was all giggly and happy the rest of the day.

≈ Who Are You? ≈

I belonged.

Have you ever felt you didn't fit in? *There's something empowering about knowing the truth of who you are.*

Nobody Like You

> *"Do not wish to be anything but who you are, and strive to be that perfectly."*
>
> – St. Francis de Sales

No one can be you better than you. They're not qualified to, called to, or equipped to be all that God created *you* to be. You are just the right combination of gifts, talents, and abilities for the job God has for you. *You were made for this moment.*

What are the implications of this revelation? If you leave this earth without fulfilling your unique purpose and completing your destiny, the world is cheated. A life that you were assigned to touch goes unchanged, a problem goes unsolved, a need unmet.

> You are just the right combination of gifts, talents, and abilities for the job God has for you.

I may see myself as inadequate, but there's another me, the one the Father sees. I want to live my life day by day to be all that He sees in me.

I attended a gathering for a well known woman in our city. Many of the guests were financially well off. They sat around talking about their extraordinary homes, extravagant vacations, and recent cosmetic surgeries. As I was quietly observing, two attractive and "extensively reconstructed" ladies came over and introduced themselves, and then said, "Honey, we've been admiring your lips from across the room!" My lips? *Really?*

At one time this kind of compliment was known as Powder Room Politics – everyone wanting something someone else has, never being satisfied with who they are. Interestingly enough, when I was younger, I walked around with my lips tucked in because kids teased me about them being too big!

In our desire to be pleasing to others we often exhaust ourselves trying to impress each other with our possessions, talents, and appearance. Seeing ourselves through a prism that is not our own can produce distorted images. If we're not careful, we'll spend a lifetime trying to be something we are not. But why strive to be a cheap version of someone else? It's far more exciting to accept the challenge of *becoming the best you there could ever possibly be*. That's something that has *never* been done before! This way of thinking abolishes any need for jealousy, because nobody can be you, or do what you do, quite like *you* can!

> *"Let every man abide in the same calling wherein he was called."*
> (1 Cor. 7:20)

Use What You've Got

David, a mere shepherd boy, convinced Saul, King of Israel, that he could kill a giant named Goliath. Saul armed David with his own armor. As honored as David must have been, David removed the armor saying, "I cannot go with these because I have not proved them." Instead, he took his own shepherd's staff in his hand along with five smooth stones and a sling shot. He went out to meet Goliath and in one shot made his target. He defeated the Philistine giant using the tools and talents he had been familiar with all along.

> You will not kill giants using someone else's armor.

You will not kill giants using someone else's armor. Don't miss the only shot you may have at success trying to fit the mold of someone or something you are not. You will be victorious in your assignment if you use the unique gifts and talents with which God has equipped you.

The Lord will not ask you why you weren't as good as or better than someone else. *In the end, God will ask why you were not "the best you."* For that, you will need to give an account (Matt. 25:22-29). What paths did you reject, what talents did you keep buried and unused, what dreams were unfulfilled? And why?

What hindered you? What excuse will be good enough when He promised to supply everything you need?

God's Assessment Tool

Corporations invest a great deal of time and money assessing their talent pool. Sometimes the talent they are seeking is right in their own back yard. Sometimes the employees themselves are unaware of their own gifts and abilities. Someone must help them to identify their hidden capabilities through self-analysis. Often tests are administered to help determine skill sets, strengths and weaknesses, career paths, and leadership potential.

Some of the greatest assessments can be found in the Bible. God asks simple questions:

1. Where Are You?

God asked this question of Adam once he fell into sin. When God asks questions, He fully knows the answer, but uses it as an opportunity for you to locate yourself. He's saying, take a look at yourself. Where are you compared to where you *should* be in life? Are you within the framework of His will, or have you gotten off track?

2. Who Told You?

On that tragic day in the garden, God asked Adam "Who told you that you were naked?" In other words, who are you listening to other than me? Who is influencing you? For us, we should take a poll of who we allow in our lives. Who has your ear? Are they distracting you, limiting you, or misdirecting you (intentionally or not)? Sort of like trying to explain to your parents why you disobeyed them and followed the crowd, then hearing them say: But, what did I tell you to do?

3. What Are You Doing Here?

Elijah, the prophet of God, was fleeing from Jezebel for his life. He became depressed and took refuge in a cave. God asked, "What are you doing here?" Elijah explained that his life was being threatened and he was feeling all alone in serving God. After a bit of drama, God asked quietly a second time, "but what are you doing *here*?" You're supposed to be in another part of the land anointing two kings to serve me and a prophet that will serve you. Oh, and by the way, although you can't see it, you are not the only person left serving me. I have seven thousand faithful remaining who have not bowed their knees to false gods. So, go!

4. What Is That In Your Hand?

"What … you mean this? This is just a simple old shepherd's rod," was basically Moses' response when God asked what he had in his hand. But God showed Moses that when he put his hand to the rod, miracles would happen. Take inventory, *everybody has something ordinary that becomes extraordinary when we use it as God commands.* As you ponder this question, you'll think of obvious things such as skills and education. But don't overlook the small things, like a simple idea, a hobby, or perhaps an old family recipe. As Ross Perot once said, all you need is one good idea to live like a king forever!

5. Who Do You Say That I Am?

Jesus' initial question to Peter was "Who do men say that I am?" Peter speculated about what others were saying about Jesus. Then Jesus personalized the question and asked him directly, "But, who do you say that I am?" Imagine Jesus looking you straight in the eyes, calling you by name and saying, "_____, who do *you* say that I am?" Recognizing God to be the Great I AM means we trust that *He is everything we need Him to be on our journey.* We can't always go by what we've heard or seen. Having that one-on-one with the Lord is very critical to our success. Is He Lord of all your life? He is willing to be, if you will allow.

One Touch

Why do we love fairytales of frog princes and swan princesses? Stories whose characters seem doomed to lives of misery and drudgery until they are kissed or touched in some magical way. Instantly, they are set free to become the glorious creatures they were destined to be. Is it because we are secretly wishing for that same kind of magic to transform our own lives? Do we somehow know that there is a well deep within us that is full of endless possibilities and potential?

> You are the keeper of the flame that burns inside of you.

What were you created with the potential or capacity to do? As you fulfill areas of your potential, you lay the framework for fulfilling your destiny. It prepares you for opportunities that line the path to your destiny. Unfulfilled potential can have negative consequences. But one touch from the Master enables the creature to emerge from the caterpillar's cocoon into the beautiful butterfly. One word from the Master caused Peter to drop his net and the woman at the well to drop her pots. Their lives were never the same again.

That touch is available to you through the potent love of a great and mighty king.

Who are you? You are the keeper of the flame that burns inside of you. Wherever your journey leads you, don't doubt in the darkness what was revealed to you in the light.

Reflections Of The Journey

- On your journey, the first enemy you will encounter is doubt and temptation. You must know who you are!

- Surviving the wilderness of doubt and temptation determines whether you move to the next level in your destiny.

- You are just the right combination of gifts, talents and abilities for the job God has for you.

- You were made for this moment!

- If you leave this earth without fulfilling your unique purpose and completing your destiny, the world is cheated.

- At your journey's end, the Lord will not ask you why you weren't as good as or better than someone else. He will ask why you were not "the best you."

- Don't doubt in the darkness what was revealed to you in the light.

The Journey Continues . . .

Exercise

It Is Written (I Am) . . .

Boldly declare God's Word and come into agreement with what it says about you.

Fill in each of the blanks with your name:

I _____, am an eternal being (not a blip on the radar screen).

I _____, am God's beloved creation, fearfully and wonderfully made.

I _____, am an earthen vessel made to house the awesome glory of God.

I _____, am given dominion over earth and every other living thing.

I _____, am made in God's image and as a speaking spirit.

I _____, am empowered to multiply His Kingdom all over this earth.

I _____, am so important that angels are assigned to guard and keep me.

I _____, am so desired that God sent His only Son to redeem me from sin and restore me back to His Kingdom.

I _____, am so valuable that Heaven wars against hell for my sake.

I _____, am Heaven sent, Heaven equipped, and Heaven blessed.

I _____, am so beloved that God knows the very number of hairs on my head.

I _____, am so interesting to God that He records everywhere I go in His book, and so precious He keeps my tears in a bottle.

That's Who I Am!

Chapter 3
Discovering Your Purpose

The task that your birth was destined for is great. Knowing your purpose on earth is crucial. Bookstores and internet sites are filled with related subject matter. So why is only one chapter of this book devoted to this important topic? Because no book, person, or assessment test can tell you what your God-ordained purpose is. You must "discover" it, as God reveals it. No short cuts. It's all a part of the journey!

A good place to begin the discovery process is to be available. God cannot send purpose into your life until you make room for it.

Collectively, we must pick up where Adam left off, being fruitful and multiplying God's glory all over the earth; establishing His Kingdom, His family, and His will here *on earth as it is in heaven*. To do that as individuals, we must impact the lives of others by using our own distinctive gifts

> God never created anything without purpose. Why should that change when He created you?

and talents. (See 1 Peter 4:10-11.) So do I have gifts and talents, you ask? Is there something I was created with the potential and capacity to do? Yes, and yes!

God never created anything without purpose. Why should that change when He created you? Everybody is called to do something. Nobody was sent just to sit. Everyone was sent to serve. Realize that you must fulfill your own unique and individual purpose on earth.

Remember this, your gift has a purpose of its own, to "Make room for you and bring you before great men" (Prov. 18:16). In other words, look beyond your gift and ask yourself: *How can my gift open doors for me to do great things for God's Kingdom?*

What did God have in mind when He created you? You may be a deliverer like Moses. Or perhaps, like Paul, you are a unifier of the body, or a builder of hope, or (your job is to fill in the blank!)

Thankfully, we have clues to guide us. Consider the following:

Steps To Discovering Your Purpose

1. Consult the Creator

When you reach a point of frustration, when you begin to question life and wonder if there is a point to your existence, God has the answer. He is the designer, creator, and master planner.

How many times have you ripped open the packaging of a newly purchased item and started assembling it, only to discover that it didn't come together quite as pictured, or didn't function as it should. Had you used the instruction manual provided by the manufacturer? Probably not. You were reluctant to do the research because that takes time. You thought you could assemble it on your own. *Uh huh.*

The great patriarchs of the Bible all had spiritual encounters that changed their lives and their destinies. Moses had his burning bush, Jacob his wrestling at Peniel, and Paul his road to Damascus. All these encounters were personal consultations with God and opportunities to submit to His will. Even the parents of Jesus and John the Baptist had encounters with God. Through prayer, you will need to experience your own face-to-face encounter to inquire, submit, and commit to the master plan, designed just for you.

Your life is no accident. You have a real purpose, a unique destiny to fulfill. If you don't know what yours is, you will pursue the wrong destiny! Only the inventor of a product can determine its functionality. You can no more *decide* your own purpose on earth than you could pick up a screw driver and expect it to grow fruit. When you are ready to discover true purpose, just follow *God's A.S.K. Plan (Ask-Seek-Knock):*

Ask – Your destiny was pre-ordained by God, who made you. Through Him you must "discover" who He especially designed you to be. Good news: He wants to reveal it to you! *Have you asked?*

Seek – Once you ask, He will take you on a journey; to transform you, to show you who He is, who you are in Him, and what He *designed and assigned* you to do.

Knock – At the appointed time, He will direct your path and order your footsteps to the doors that lead to your future. He will open doors that no man can shut.

> *"Ask and it will be given to you; seek and you will find; knock and the door will be opened to you. For everyone who asks receives; the one who seeks finds; and to the one who knocks, the door will be opened."*
>
> (Matt. 7: 7-8)

Isn't it time you inquired? Consult the Creator.

2. What are Your Gifts?

God gives the gift that the gift may be given.

Some people go their whole lives waiting for their gifts to show up. No need to wait. The gifts are already there, although they may be lying dormant. They simply need to be activated, stirred up, set in motion.

> God gives the gift that the gift may be given.

> *"Wherefore I put thee in remembrance that thou stir up the gift of God, which is in thee by the putting on of my hands."*
>
> (2 Tim. 1:6)

So, how do you recognize and identify *your* gifts? Whatever you were born to do, you are gifted or equipped to do. He has called you to it. Whatever you were born to do, you are probably already doing on some level. Consider your career, ministry, or relationships. Something you do (or have done), is representative of your innate potential. It may have been something on a small scale that you enjoyed, or something that came naturally to you, or something others regularly complimented you on, but *the gift was speaking to you.*

For some, the gift is obvious, such as music, athletics, and fine arts. Other less visible gifts are often overlooked or simply unrecognized as being gifts. Examples of these are oration, leadership, counsel, administration, craftsmanship and hospitality. What Moses thought was a simple rod in his hand, God used to perform some of the greatest miracles in the Bible, and bring about the deliverance of a great people. Today, God still uses ordinary people to carry out His plans. What's in your hand? What makes you unique? What can you do better than most people?

Be sure to enter your response in the "Discovering My Purpose" exercise at the end of the chapter.

If your gift is alive in you it will prosper wherever you go; from the classroom to the boardroom, from the pulpit to the grocery store. The Kingdom of God is *everywhere!*

> *"A gift is as a precious stone in the eyes of him that hath it: Whithersoever it turneth, it prospereth."*
>
> (Prov.17:8)

> **Whatever you do, do it with purpose!**

You may be blessed with multiple gifts. Along the pathway to purpose, you will want to grow in the direction of your dominant gift. Whatever you do, do it with purpose!

≈ Discovering Your Purpose ≈

What Is Your "That"?

Think of a new company starting up, or ministry, or community center. No one has been assigned to do anything yet. What would you sign up to do? Where would you say you'd be most effective? Think to yourself, "I can't do this, but I can sure do *that*." Where could you make the most difference? What would "that" be?

List your "That's" in the chapter exercise.

Suppose a company has hired a talented pool of candidates but needs to develop a training manual. Could you do that? The contractor builds beautiful homes but has no salesmanship or marketing abilities. Do you? The event coordinator planned a lovely banquet but certainly is not a cook. Could you cater it? You're all about fitness, good exercise, and healthy eating habits. Can you help your five co-workers who are constantly lamenting over their weight-loss struggles? Your marriage survived ten tumultuous years before you and your spouse finally learned how to become one. Have you noticed the divorce rate lately? Help!

There's a popular TV show that features a nanny who helps parents bring order to their households and learn how to raise healthy, happy children. Parents of small children seem to be hungry for this information. They are praying for a similar type show on raising teens. Maybe you know the secret. Your mentoring or nurturing skills may be just what are needed to raise up a righteous generation of Kingdom kids.

You don't know anything about medicine, but you can repair anything, grow anything, or organize anything. Maybe you've found your "that."

You will know you are in your place of purpose when your gift opens up and begins to meet the needs of others.

On the other hand, if others don't benefit from what you do, or it always seems to be a struggle and doesn't improve or get easier with practice, this "that" is not your gift.

> You will know you are in your place of purpose when your gift opens up and begins to meet the needs of others.

A Luminous Gift

Celebrities are gifted and empowered with a voice, or what some call a platform. The "way" you achieved such stature (acting, singing, politics) may not be quite as important as the "why." That you are able to command an audience is not so much that your voice will be heard, as it is that God has graced you to have a means through which His voice may be heard *through* you.

A common misconception is that people whose talents have made it into the limelight are undoubtedly fulfilling their life's purpose. Not necessarily so!

> Moving in gifts does not equal moving in purpose.

Moving in gifts does not equal moving in purpose. We must be careful not to run after our gift. The gift is there to serve our purpose, not the other way around.

Hence, many celebrities experience emptiness even though they have achieved wealth and fame. That lack of fulfillment is an indicator that there is more to our existence than what the world offers. It's a reminder that our gifts only create the platform or "make room" for us to stand before great men, and move in our purpose. So when we have the spotlight, that is the opportunity to impact God's Kingdom. How? By saying or doing whatever He called you for in this hour. That is what is He is waiting for you to discover in Him.

The only thing that brings total fulfillment is being in the center of God's will for your life.

> The only thing that brings total fulfillment is being ian the center of God's will for your life.

Heart of a Champion

Perhaps you are an athlete. If so, you have the heart of a champion. Sports after all, are designed to overcome obstacles on the way to victory in pursuit of a goal. As an athlete, you are not just called to the sports arena, but you are gifted in recognizing and reaching other champions in all walks of life. A lot of people don't know how to win at what they do. Often the missing ingredient in bringing their vision to pass is goal-setting, strategizing, and winning. Successful athletes are naturals at this! Could it be that your skills are transferable from the court to the Kingdom, from the stadium to the pew? Perhaps you can help others discover how to strategize, win, and gain victories based on your own experiences. *Speak to the winner in all of us.*

No doubt, true athletes are fearless competitors. Beneath the uniform beats the heart of a warrior. The athlete's performance is an outward manifestation of the warrior within. It is much like David, who used the same warrior characteristics he exhibited in his youth (when he slew the lion, the bear, and the giant with a shepherd's sling) as he did as king, leading his nation back to God. Perhaps athletes of today are also called to be warriors in the spirit and defenders of the gospel.

Never underestimate the heart of a champion!

3. What Do You Love?

Think of what you are passionate about. What do you love doing? What could you do every day and never get tired of it? What do you dream of or envision yourself doing? What could you talk about almost continuously? My how time flies when you're moving in purpose! Where does the energy come from? It's a promise of provision:

> *"Blessed are those whose strength is in you; whose hearts are set on the pilgrimage (journey) ... They go from strength to strength,"*
>
> (Ps. 84:5-7, NIV)

The Lord gives strength to those who are focused on their journey!

Now think of *who* you are passionate about. If given the resources and ability, what group of people do you have a desire to enlighten, empower, or set free? What are you supposed to give them, help them accomplish, or overcome?

Find something you love and live it.

Find something you love and give it.
Find a way to take what you love and connect it to the needs of others.

4. Spiritual Strengths

Purpose can emerge as spiritual strengths – areas where you are more spiritually adept than others.

If you enter a room and people say "here comes trouble," you know you are not walking in purpose. But when you enter an atmosphere where people are troubled and they lift their heads and think, "here comes peace," purpose has been unveiled. People whose hearts are heavy and filled with despair should cry out "Thank God, hope just showed up" when you walk into the room. *Sometimes people see purpose in you long before you see it in yourself. They are drawn to it.* What do people generally call on you for? A wise word? A compassionate ear? What can they count on you for? Praise? Encouragement? Do you speak wisdom where there is no insight or focus?

Do people who are downcast get a pick me up after talking to you? You may be called to exhort and encourage. Where the atmosphere is filled with darkness and confusion, does your presence and conversation consistently bring revelation and truth? When things are in disarray, do you tend to restore order and organization? Some of these qualities are befitting one who is capable of upholding law and order or even judging the people, like Deborah. Or you may be the voice or intercessor for the oppressed, like Moses. Or perhaps like David, your music breathes worship into people's dry places. In a dismal, unproductive environment do you spark creativity and cause fresh ideas to flow? When harsh words and attitudes separate and divide, are you a mediator or repairer of the breach?

Hmmm…Who will they say just walked in the room when you show up?

> Sometimes people see purpose in you long before you see it in yourself. They are drawn to it.

5. Dominant or Prevailing Ideas and Interests

Your purpose can be evident in dreams and ideas that keep coming back to you.

Be sure to list the things you commonly get ideas about in the chapter exercise.

Some childhood dreams and ideas are so prevalent that they stay with us into adulthood. When we were little girls, I was the unwilling subject for all of Sister's health and beauty creations: oatmeal facials, coffee hair conditioner, and let's not forget the ammonia sinus treatment (my nostrils still burn in cold weather)! I pause to say that Sister's given name is Tamara, but it is the way we address each other, having been so close. Anyway, the point is, she had a desire then to impart health and nutrition. Later on, she became the owner of Body Beautiful Products, a natural skin care and weight loss company. After all those years of experimentation, she finally created a product with global appeal. Her stretch mark removal product is in demand all around the world. Yes, I said stretch marks. Don't hate—appreciate!

After working at a health food store for just a short time, customers began to personally request her because of her ability to discern health issues and determine the appropriate herbs and supplements. Recently, when she began teaching classes again, a lady showed up and said, "Remember me? You helped me ten years ago. Can you help me now?" And for Christmas, all Sister ever wanted as a little girl was dishes and house wares. It's no wonder she is such a wonderful homemaker today.

You probably haven't thought much about the things you found interest and pleasure in as a child, but maybe you should. If you are a parent, you will also want to begin recording observations of your children's gifts, strengths, and areas of interest to prepare them for their future.

As for me, I always enjoyed singing and songwriting. Was it just a hobby or a hint at my divine purpose?

God Gives The Gift ...

I'd heard it said that I was often too weak to cry as a baby. Yet, before I walked or talked, Mom knew that I was feeling sick by the same melancholy tune I hummed as she held me against her shoulder and patted my back. As a little girl, I made up songs about things I saw around me, like the happy song about the white pigeon that used to perch on our window sill in the housing projects. But as an adult, as much as I loved to sing, I had doubts that music was something God wanted to use me in.

> God does not accept returns on His gifts.

I knew that my vocal abilities did not begin to compare to the likes of Mariah, Patti, Celine, Yolanda, or the incomparable Whitney. But each time I tried to give it back to God, He refused it. I found that God does not accept returns on His gifts.

One day, I sat at my kitchen table in tears, apologizing to God for having focused so much time and energy on music. Surely my attention had been misdirected and caused me to miss whatever it was God had truly purposed me to do. I made a decision to put music and singing on the shelf. I can't tell you how good it felt to release the music thing to God. More than that, I was excited to finally find out what it was God was going to reveal to me as my *true* Kingdom purpose.

The next day I went to work feeling light on my feet and happier than I'd felt in a long time. My good friend and co-worker, who was organizing the employee awards banquet, asked who I thought should give the invocation. The person who immediately came to mind, was someone I didn't know very well and hadn't seen in a long time. "That's funny," Antoinette said, "she came by earlier today and said she'd be back later."

Sure enough, Karen came back. She saw that Antoinette and I were engaged in conversation, so she waited quietly, leaning against the edge of my desk. Suddenly, out of the blue, Karen turned to me and blurted, "You write songs." I looked at Antoinette, who just shrugged her shoulders as if to say, "I didn't tell her anything." I couldn't even look at Karen. I knew I had been busted, so I just put both hands up as if to surrender to whatever I was about to hear from God. Then, the word of the Lord came to me through Karen saying:

"Your hands are anointed to write songs for the world to hear. You've been feeling that the gift you have is not enough. God says it's more than enough."

It's a good thing I was sitting down. I slumped over on my desk and sobbed. It amazed me that God sent His answer so quickly (not that I had asked). I felt like a fugitive trying to escape my assignment, and Karen was a bounty hunter sent by God to arrest me and to stop me from making a terrible mistake. Sometimes we just need to reach a point of surrender. That was mine.

Perhaps there have been times when the Lord sent someone your way, but you did not recognize him or her as His messenger. It is so important that we always have an ear to hear. Without a doubt, God had heard my cry. But hearing me say I was abandoning His gift inside of me was enough to make Him rise up from the throne and say, "Somebody go right now and tell my child not to walk away from her gift and endanger her purpose!"

That's how important purpose is to God.

... That The Gift May Be Given

A few weeks later, it became clear why God needed me focused on purpose. He had lined up a little assignment for me. While attending a meeting for the Habitat for Humanity Jimmy Carter Work Project, the Lord impressed upon me to write a song for the occasion. What I did not know was that the Houston Chamber of Commerce had been looking for a song for this occasion, preferably written by a celebrity. Instead, God sent me. When I walked in and played the song entitled *"One Heart, One Hand, One House at a Time,"* a woman from the Chamber literally leaped from her chair and kissed me on the cheek (we had never met before)! The song was featured during the international closing ceremonies with an audience of 6000. That's when I recalled God's word to me, *a song for the world to hear*! Backstage, I met Millard Fuller, the founder of Habitat International. He asked my permission to include the song in Habitat's international songbook, with proceeds going toward the elimination of poverty through affordable housing. A no brainer. And a prophecy fulfilled.

Let's review, shall we? Did the gift make room for me and bring me before great men according to Proverbs 18:16? Did it create access for Kingdom work to be done? Indeed! But just weeks before, had I truly abandoned my purpose, none of this would have become a reality.

A Word In Season

A few years later I would be tested again.

It was spring, such a lovely season, and I was charged with coordinating my church's Ladies Luncheon. The previous year had been a mentally and emotionally exhausting year for me, filled with much disappointment and too much on my plate. I'd had an especially rough winter. With the hint of spring in the air, the ladies had elected to create an atmosphere of "High Tea." Since I was the Mistress of Ceremonies, someone had flopped a big hat on my head and some frilly gloves. Bah humbug! What I really wanted was to sit somewhere and do nothing, just lay back and disappear into the wallpaper. Everything I had tried lately seemed to fail, including my brief marriage. And why did God keep telling me He wants to do something musically? Well, if it really was God, something more would have happened by now.

Well, I had a choice. I could stand and watch the world go by and become a victim of my own circumstances, or I could believe God.

A prophetic word then came to me in two forms. (One definition of a prophetic word is from Jer. 1:10, that it uproots what is not God and plants what is, breaks down what is not God and builds what is. It may also confirm, stir, warn, amplify, or encourage you to walk out God's plan for your life).

The first, and most unlikely, was through the lyrics to soul singer Maxwell's *"Lifetime,"* a song about choosing to let our lives pass us by, or making the effort to work on it during this lifetime. I played this song over and over again, because I needed to answer the question: Would I let it all pass me by?

The other word that came to me blew my mind. It was given by the guest speaker for this High Tea luncheon I didn't want to be at! She did not know me, my background, my insecurities or my gifts. It was recorded and transcribed:

> *"Girl. We command songs, music, tapes, television, recordings—come out! Come out! Come out! Come! Alleluia. I hear this word for you.*
>
> *"Who said it? Who said you couldn't? Who said you weren't good enough? Who told you that? Who told you you couldn't do it? Who said it's for somebody else, and not for you? Who said that you could not be holy? Who said you couldn't be full of glory? Who said you couldn't be on television? Who said you couldn't be on radio? Who said your voice could not cover the earth and your praise could not be heard from nation to nation? Who said it's over and it's finished? Who said - who told you you were nobody? Who told you you were little? Who told you they don't need your songs and your voice and your anointing?*
>
> *"Wasn't me, saith the Spirit of God. Was not me! I said, magnify the Lord. Bless me, praise my name, exalt me and, if you exalt me I cannot help but exalt and lift you.*
>
> *"God has said He's told you over and over and over and over things you should be doing. And you continue to let yourself be pushed back, shut up. Doing the service of God. Wounded, offended. But because you held in there and stayed, the Father says I open your prison door. Now come out. Come!*
>
> *"You are so vital. You're vital to the ministry. You're vital to the Kingdom of God and the enemy just keeps telling you you ain't nothing and you ain't nobody and nobody don't care and*

nobody don't want you and you ain't good for nothin'. Uh-uh, uh-uh, he lied to you. He is the Father of Lies and he lied to you.

"And you know when that little thing came in there - that low self-esteem. You know when and where and we going right back there. We snatch it. We cut it. Come on, come on…and we let it go. It was not your fault and stop blaming yourself. Alleluia. An enemy.

"Who said it? Who said it? Was not me! Was not me! I said you're holy. I said you're full of glory. I said it, I! I! I! I! I said it! Who said it?"

Whew!

Did you hear that big "boom" sound? That was my mind being blown! Maybe this was a word for some of you too. In response to this word from the Lord, I got to work that year. I began by completing unfinished songs. It was hard. Many storms and distractions came my way. But I had decided not to "continue to let myself be pushed back, shut up and offended." I did produce and complete my first CD entitled *My Destiny*. The gift was stirred up within me by the laying on of hands.

I hope you see my experience as an example for you. Once you awaken to your God- given purpose, nothing can keep you from it. Circumstances cannot keep you from it. Opinions of others cannot keep you from it. Once you discover your purpose and get into agreement with what God says about you, you will never be the same.

It's All About You—Not!

You were made to impact someone else's life.

There's a seed on the inside of you. At some point in our lives God births a passion inside to achieve something great and you begin to desire your destiny. The gifts inside of you, no matter how small they seem to you, are valuable to the Kingdom of God. You only need to allow the Word of God to come down on the inside and nurture that seed, making it possible for you to conceive and cause an awesome thing to be born of you.

The dream inside your heart, God put it there. But the dreams, the gifts, the talents—they are not for *you*. Their intended purpose is to bless others through you. You were designed to be a mighty river—a conduit for God's blessings to flow through to reach wherever and whomever He wants. Remember, God desires to use us to establish His Kingdom in the earth.

> There is no more exciting life to live than one consumed with purpose!

There is no more exciting life to live than one consumed with purpose!

Reflections Of The Journey

- No book, person, or assessment test can tell you what your God-ordained purpose is. You must "discover" it, as God reveals it.

- A good place to begin is to be available.

- God never created anything without purpose. Why should that change when He created you?

- Moving in gifts does not equal moving in purpose.

- Your purpose can be evident in dreams and ideas that keep coming back to you.

- You will know you are in your place of purpose when your gift opens up and begins to meet the needs of others.

- The purpose of your gift is to "make room for you and bring you before great men," creating access for you to do Kingdom work.

The Journey Continues . . .

Exercise

Discovering My Purpose

A good place to begin the discovery process is to identify what's familiar to you.

Please complete the following:

What's in your Hand? Identify something that makes you unique; something perhaps ordinary to you, but that you can do better than most people:

What is your That? Think to yourself, *"I can't do this, but I can sure do that"*. What would *"that"* be?

Think of things you are passionate about. What do you love doing? What is it you could do every day and never get tired of?

Think back to your childhood likes and interests. What did you most enjoy doing?

What group of people do you have a desire to enlighten, empower, or set free?

Describe an idea that keeps coming back to you:

> *"Man is man because he is free to operate within the framework of his destiny. He is free to deliberate, to make decisions, and to choose between alternatives. He is distinguished from animals by his freedom to do evil or to do good and to walk the high road of beauty or tread the low road of ugly degeneracy."*
>
> –Martin Luther King, Jr.

Chapter 4
Moving Toward Your Destiny

Choice Or Chance? - What Is To Be Is Up To Me

Destiny is different than fate. Fate happens no matter what. *Destiny awaits you, but you must choose it and move toward it.*

The way your life began wasn't up to you. You didn't choose your parents, date of birth, city, gender or even your name. But where you go from here *is* your choice. The future God has for you is not limited by your past, your education level, or what side of the tracks you were born on.

Why complain about the family you were born into? Sadly, you may have been the product of rape or incest, or born into poverty to a prostitute mother or drug-addicted father. You are not responsible nor held accountable for that. You cannot choose your DNA, but you can choose your destiny. It's not about how you came here, but it has everything to do with how you go on from here. This is *your* race. It wasn't given to the

> You cannot choose your DNA, but you can choose your destiny.

swift or to the strong; it was given to you, in your present state. Run your race. Run with patience. Run with passion.

Of course, you don't *have* to walk in your destiny. God created humans with free will. He says, "I have set before you blessings and curses, life and death. Choose life" (Deut. 30:19). So you will succeed or fail based on your own choices. Where you are today is largely based on the decisions made yesterday. Your future successes or failures will be based on the decisions you are making today, right now. Within this very hour you may have just decided between fried and baked, or between video games and a book, or even speaking in anger versus holding your peace. When you act on your own choices, you define your own future.

You might be thinking: Why choose to walk in my destiny? Why not leave it to chance, and just let life happen to me? Because when life just happens to you, you are a victim. When you choose to pursue your destiny, you become a champion!

So, is there more than one way, one pathway to my destiny?

Yes, but the one you pick could be a lonely and dangerous one. When we're off God's chosen path, we are outside of his best for us. As my grandma often said, "God will take you the easiest way you'll come!"

Opportunity Is Everywhere

News Flash: The sky is no longer the limit. There are now footprints on the moon (duh)!

Many opportunities line the path to your destiny. But *not every open door is intended for you to walk through.* Otherwise, how would you accept several job opportunities or admissions to various colleges at the same time?

When you don't acknowledge purpose or give attention to the gifts inside you, you won't be able to recognize the open door when it comes your way. You'll refuse a certain position on the job because it doesn't offer a raise or prestigious title, instead of recognizing it as a developmental opportunity that's directly along the path to your destiny. When the dream job finally comes along, you may look back and realize that you couldn't have qualified for it without the experiences you gained, or people you connected with along the way.

Don't get nervous because your path doesn't seem to be going in a straight and tidy direction. What journey does? There are times when you have to go left to go right. There is something you need that's off the beaten path, perhaps some pre-requisite that will qualify you for a future opportunity you aren't aware of or planning for. Or, perhaps God has ordained a life you must touch along the way.

One summer, I dreamed about doors nearly every night. Most of them looked like doors I was very familiar with, like the ones in my own home. But as I tried the conventional method of turning the doorknob, the door would not open. Finally, I saw a beautiful Japanese woman who said, "Door of opportunity is now open!" Then, whoosh! The panels 'slid' open. No door knob needed.

The door to your future will probably not look the way you envisioned it would. Every miracle God performed in the Bible came with simple instructions. So simple, they were easy to miss because they didn't make sense to the human mind.

> The door to your future will probably not look the way you envisioned it would.

Some good questions to ask are: How does the opportunity fit with my mission, vision and goals? Does it hinder me in the assignment God has for me? Does it add to or take away from it? *Sometimes distractions are masked as opportunities.* They look good and sound enticing but only throw you off track and slow you down. As you continually devote yourself to a life of purpose, you will gradually develop an internal compass and be drawn toward people and opportunities that align with your vision.

Follow The Favor!

There is one last point to consider when recognizing open doors. Sometimes the answers to the following questions can be your determining factor: Where is it that you are appreciated and valued? Who is celebrating you, developing you and promoting you? Follow the favor!

When God's favor is on your life, wonderful things will happen to you and for you:

- Favor is better than money.
- Favor is the divine current that carries you to your destiny (my daily prayer).
- Favor opens doors for you that are hidden from others.
- Favor does for you what talent, skills & education cannot.
- Favor attracts right people to your life.
- Favor will cancel a debt or obligation and restore your good name.
- Favor will catapult you to the top of the organizational chart.
- Favor will cause not enough to be more than enough.
- Favor opens doors that no man can shut.
- Favor connects you to the one person, organization or ministry with the key to unlocking your destiny.

> Because you have chosen to commit to the journey – Favor is going to explode in your life!

I could go on and on, but the point to be made is that the journey does come with supernatural perks. Just remember, it's through no goodness of your own, but the favor of God. Every time I recognize God's favor moving in my life I pause to acknowledge it. (Gratitude increases the flow).

Friend, because you have chosen to commit to the journey – *Favor is going to explode in your life!*

Access Granted

Living in Austin, Texas, was beautiful. The greenery, lakes, and rolling hills reminded me of Pennsylvania. The new regional office facility was tucked away in the hills in an area that had been preserved for wildlife (mostly deer). By agreement, when the company built on the land, certain portions remained undeveloped. This meant the walkways around the building weren't designed in straight, convenient paths from the parking lots.

As a resident employee, I had electronic key access to all entrances around the building. But visitors from field offices had to walk the long path around to the front entrance. As the head tour guide for the grand opening, I recall explaining all this to our management and employees. But later, when I relocated, I was asked to turn in my resident key. Whenever I visited Austin, I dreaded taking the scenic route around to the visitor's entrance, plus showing ID at the front desk.

One day, my boss figured I was traveling to Austin frequently enough to warrant restoring my resident key privileges. I went online and filled out the all-important key access request form, carefully stating my reasons for special approval status. My boss approved it and forwarded it on to security. The email reply was instant:

"You have always had access to this facility". That was it. No explanation.

What? I couldn't believe I'd been taking the nature trail to Timbuktu, when I had direct access all this time to the doors closest to me! But then a deeper thought came: *What other doors have you had access to in life and didn't know it?* Where have you been watching others go before you, not knowing you had the same favor, rights, and privileges? Where else in life have you been pleading to get into, showing ID and trying to prove who you are?

You have already been granted access!

Preparation – *Go Slow To Go Fast*

What's that you say? I actually have to prepare for it? Doesn't success just happen? You've asked the question, now expect the answer. When you truly expect something grand to show up in your life, prepare accordingly. *You must get ready for greatness!* If you received notice that the person you admired most in life was going to be a guest in your home for the next three days, what would you do to prepare? Prepare for your opportunity by making room in your life. Remove all the clutter. Clean out negative thoughts and distractions like noise or busy, unfruitful activity. The environment must be just right for this encounter. Create the atmosphere that is conducive and necessary.

The biblical story of Queen Esther teaches us that each day of our lives should be lived in a state of preparation, education, and development, so that when our appointed time comes, we'll be ready.

Take time to prepare. How long? It can't truly be measured in terms of months or years, but more like seasons. But when things do begin to happen, they sometimes take off pretty quickly. No time to stop and figure out how to do things or fix things. Go slow now to go fast when opportunity comes.

Remember the parable of the wise and foolish virgins? All ten were aware of the impending opportunity, but didn't know when it would actually occur. The five wise purchased oil for their lamps, just in case the event occurred at night. But the five foolish took a chance, and lo and behold, it happened at midnight. Instead of entering the door, they went scurrying about to find oil. Eventually they obtain it, but it was too little too late. The door of opportunity was shut. In this scenario, think of the oil in your lamp as whatever you need to sacrifice or invest in to equip you for your journey—finances, education, certifications, preparing a business plan, resolving health issues, developing a product, sharpening a skill, consulting with experts, and even adjusting your schedule to make room in your life for your opportunity. Get your house in order!

The teacher speaks little during the actual test, but it is during times of preparation that He speaks most. Take special note of Scriptures He is giving you now. Write them down and do not discard them. You will need to refer back to them later.

Take care to do those things now, lest you be unprepared and the door be shut on your opportunity.

These Shoes Are Killing Me!

With comfort in mind, we choose shoes that aren't too large or too small for us, but that fit just right. But in life, sometimes it's good to choose the shoes you hope to fill. They may be uncomfortable at first, but just keep walking—you'll grow into them. Those shoes that fit just right or too tight are killing you. They keep you from growing and aspiring to be greater than you are.

During the grand opening of Lakewood Church, Pastor Joel Osteen reflected on his early days in ministry, stepping into the pulpit after his famed father Pastor John Osteen had passed away. To give himself confidence, he wore his father's shoes! He did this because it made him feel like his father was with him. However, he soon realized that God was with him, just as He had been with his father. Their story reminds me so much of Moses and Joshua. After Moses' death, the Lord said to Joshua, "As I was with Moses, so shall I be with you."

> *"Every place that the sole of your foot shall tread upon, that have I given unto you, as I said unto Moses."*
>
> Josh. 1:3

Who do you admire for their achievements, integrity and leadership? *Whose well-shod feet do you want to model yours after?*

The Journey Begins

To fully prepare, you must:

- Acknowledge the past.
- Assess where you are.
- Plan for the future.

As you acknowledge your past, you will visit the reflection pool (be honest with what you see), look for common themes that run through your past (same mistakes, same people), and decide what will you leave behind.

Then let go! The past can be very seductive.

Please let go.

To assess where you are, you will identify your assets, accomplishments, and support systems.

And to plan for the future, you will reflect on what you want most in life, who you want to become, and taking your first steps toward reaching your goal.

Please take time to address these areas by completing *"The Journey Begins" self-assessment at the end of the chapter.*

A Letter To My Past – The Year Ago Test

Do you still have the same problem you had a year ago? Are you still complaining about the same things, or perhaps even more? Take a moment to identify what has changed and what has not.

> Make a start toward some small piece of your dream today.

Have you in any way moved in purpose, according to the plans God has for you? I challenge you this year to remove from your vocabulary "some day" or "one of these days." Make a start toward some small piece of your dream *today*.

Throughout the book, you will write three letters to yourself and others. To yourself, to help acknowledge and release the past; to share with others, to hold you accountable to your goals; and to your future, to define where you want the journey to take you.

Take a moment to write the first letter, using the "Letter to my Past," template at the end of the chapter. A year from now, that letter should be old news!

Are You Ready?

Which best describes you:

> "I dreamed of a thousand new paths. I awoke and walked my old one."

Or,

> "I'll not go where the path has already been laid. I'll go where there is no path and leave a trail."

I can't give you the answers but if I can get you to ask yourself the right questions, the answers will come.

- Are you walking in your destiny?
- Do you truly desire your destiny?
- Have you received it?
- Do you celebrate it?
- Will you embrace your destiny?

- Will you guard it?
- What if you were guaranteed to succeed? (He will crown your efforts with success.)
- How would you celebrate? You are not allowed to "Sit this one out!"

"Neglect not the gift that is in thee..."

(1 Tim. 4:14)

You know, recording artists always say they remember where they were the first time they heard themselves on the radio. I was on my way to work, stuck in a traffic jam when I heard: "It's time to move, y'all. So check this out!" Jeri P. Beasley of KYOK radio was playing the first cut from my debut CD, *Moving Toward My Destiny*.

Yes, it is time to move. Time to set some things in motion.

It's *your* destiny. Pursue it with passion! Ladies, put on your dancin' shoes. Gentlemen, start your engines! But wait, before you turn the key in the ignition, one final question.

Are you really ready to go?

> It's your destiny. Pursue it with passion!

Reflections Of The Journey

- Fate happens no matter what. Destiny awaits you, but you must choose it and move toward it.

- You cannot choose your DNA, but you can choose your destiny.

- When you act on your own choices you define your own future.

- The door to your future will probably not look the way you envisioned it would.

- Not every open door is intended for you to walk through.

- The teacher speaks little during the actual test, but it is during times of preparation that He speaks most.

- Remove from your vocabulary "someday" or "one of these days."

- It's your destiny – pursue it with passion!

The Journey Continues . . .

Exercise

The Journey Begins - Self Assesement

To fully prepare for the journey you must acknowledge the past, assess where you are, and prepare for the future.

Acknowledge Your Past:

Visit the reflection pool. Be honest with yourself. In your own words, describe *who* you see.

Are there common themes that run through your past (same mistakes, same people)?

Look at childhood pictures of yourself and notice when the smiles stopped. Then remember why. (Parents divorced, moved away from friends and relatives, gained weight, abused, etc.):

If you could change one thing about your past, what would it be?

Assess Where You Are:

What are your assets (education, talent, experience, personality)? It may help to ask others.

Are you spiritually grounded? _____ Yes _____ No

What are your 3 best accomplishments?

Do you have a good support system? Please identify:

Plan For The Future:

What do you want most in life?

When you look back on this year, what is the most important thing you want to be able to say you accomplished (reduced debt, took a class, joined a gym)?

What has <u>got</u> to change in 2 years or less?

Where do you want to be in the next five years?

Decide how <u>you</u> define success:

Letter To My Past

In your own words, acknowledge mistakes, regrets, and decisions that have led you to where you are today. Forgive those who have caused you pain. Forgive yourself. Declare that you will no longer live in the shadows of yesterday. Bid farewell and tell your past you are *moving on!*

_____

_____

_____

_____

_____

_____

_____

_____

_____

_____

_____

_____

_____

_____

_____   _____
Signature   Date

Part II
The Adventure

Chapter 5

Survivor: Ain't No Mountain

On the popular reality TV show "Survivor," average Americans become castaways and endure extreme challenges in some of the most unforgiving places on the earth. My own reality was just as treacherous, minus the Hollywood backdrop. It was much like the children of Israel, who wandered through the wilderness, facing steep mountains, dark valleys and giants in the land.

Let's journey back to my reality, to witness the assignment the enemy had on my life from my birth, and the unveiling of God's purpose through the pain.

People often long for the carefree days and joys of childhood.

Me, not so much.

Cast Down But Not Forsaken

"Don't cry, Sammie. She's still a beautiful baby."

"But look at her face. She'll have to live with that for the rest of her life. She's marked."

"Naw, naw, sis. She'll be remembered," Jessy soothed.

"Yeah, who could forget? Why would God give her something' like that? So people can tease her all her life?"

"You watch. That birthmark is going to become a beauty mark. She'll be recognized by it, known by it. You watch."

Mom told me about this conversation with her brother when I was older and began to ask about my appearance. Questions like: "Why is my face different than other kids?" And "Will I ever be able to wash it off?" You see, neighborhood kids said it was dirt. Some adults gossiped, saying that I had been burned. But Mom had more to worry about than the way I looked when I was born. She worried that I wasn't going to live.

My birth was unplanned and also several weeks premature. I lay in a hospital incubator, fighting for my life, for a month. Once home, I was too puny and frail to even part my lips for food or drink. Growing up, I was plagued with colds, sore throats, sinus infections, nosebleeds, fainting spells, and more. As I grew older, the anemia that plagued me grew severe, bringing on hallucinations. Pain was my constant companion.

Hold Hands And Run!

Mom's dry cleaner shop was across the street from the old post office. That's where she taught my big sister and me how to cross busy streets. "If one of you girls gets hit by a car, you'd better both get hit!" In other words, we were not to leave the other behind. "Now hold hands and run!"

Somehow, Mom convinced the school administrators to let me start school a year early so her girls could be together. Already small for my age, I was an easy target for the class bullies. They called me lots of cruel names, but the most hurtful was "bag-a-bones." That's all I was in their eyes. Not a person, just a bag of bones. I felt worthless and empty, like there was nothing inside, just an ugly bag of dry bones.

My battle with low self-esteem had officially begun.

Sister and I were attacked almost daily. We would hear the thunderous sound of footsteps and turn to see the whole school coming toward us over the hill side. We held hands and ran like the wind. They circled around us like vultures, walked on the backs of our shoes, pulled our hair, and knocked our books to the ground. They assaulted us all the way home, but they dared not climb the front porch stairs. Not since Mom told one girl, "If you woman enough to step foot on my porch, you woman enough for me to kick your (bleep!)."

This was beyond bullying. It was an all out attack on the Gaynor girls. The Clairton police often escorted us home. Once inside, I hid in closets, where I would make up songs and let music take me away until I felt strong enough to come out. At night, I cried and sang myself to sleep. Sometimes, Sister told me bedtime stories in which I was the brave, beautiful heroine who could face down those same evil villains and emerge victorious.

The next day, we licked our wounds and returned to school. And the next day, and the next.

God Places Special People Along The Path

Battered by bullying and sickness made childhood difficult, but the sore throats were the worst, often with swollen glands. I couldn't talk, or even swallow water. Only Sister could understand me, and she became my interpreter. Sometimes, even she would tire of me being sick because she had no one to play with. We'd bundle up and head outside to build a snowman, but by the time we rolled the snowman's bottom, I was already sick and had to go back inside. Sister would prop me up inside by the window and tap whenever she made progress with the snowman, like finding something to use for his nose or eyes. When she finished, she jumped up and down in the snow. She had to jump for both of us. She literally was my strength when I was weak, and my voice when I couldn't speak. I was glad she was along for my journey.

Twins No More

Being just ten months apart, Mom always dressed us as twins. Sister did all my talking, I just looked down, too shy to look strangers in the eye. Anything I was afraid to do, I would hide behind her so she could go first. She'd have to report back to me saying it's okay, you can come out now. But in fifth grade they placed us in separate classrooms. Oh my! How could I get along without Sister? Who would talk for me now?

We were no longer one.

High School Daze

I was optimistic about high school, thinking kids would be more mature and I could stop worrying about fights. But my first week, as I walked through the senior high school level toward the junior high staircase, I heard voices behind me. As the voices got closer, I heard a senior girl say, "Look at her. Walking all reared back like she's some model!" She was mimicking the way I walked, so I turned around to see what "walk" she meant. Big mistake. She punched me square in the face and the whole bunch of them ran off laughing. (Oh how I wish I was making all this up).

As the fights continued in high school, I wondered – will this war ever end?

PG (Parental Guidance Required)

As a young girl, I was slow to develop physically, and even when I did it was barely noticeable. Sister, on the other hand was a ravishing beauty even as a little girl, turning the heads of older males. Once, she was lured into a dark stairwell by a male cousin and molested, then victimized again when Mom refused to believe her. About that same time, we were excited to hear that Mom's friend was moving back to town with her daughter Dee Dee. She had always been such fun to play with. But when she arrived, something had changed. Her conversation was about boys, sex, and cigarettes. That's when we learned the awful truth that rocked us all to the core. Little Dee Dee was being sexually molested by her own father. Her innocence had been destroyed.

So had Sister's. She became confused, not knowing if she was a woman or still a child. Should she wear pigtails or pumps? Without anyone to answer her questions, she soon became a teenage mother.

Fortunately, boys didn't pay attention to my skinny little self. Or so I believed. Apparently, my slowly developing body was noticeable to some, like the friend of my brother's who came to the house frequently and tried to molest me whenever my brother left the room. And the adolescent cousin who decided while I was sleeping over, to slip under the sheets and let his fingers do a little walking. I pretended to be asleep while locking my knees tightly together. I prayed he would go away. He did.

Parents, guard your children! Be careful who you let get close to them. Think of who else may be in the house when you allow them to visit or sleep over. You just can't be too careful.

Ain't No Mountain

God calls His people to the mountain top for instruction, demonstration, and communion with Him. Moses, Jesus, and His disciples were among those who met God on mountain tops. But the Christian life is not leaping from mountaintop to mountaintop. Even in the best seasons of your life you will face adversity or something that blocks access to your dream.

Along your journey, you will face many mountains. A mountain is something that has exalted itself in your life, and is standing between you and your promise.

> A mountain is something that has exalted itself in your life, and is standing between you and your promise.

Let's go back in time again to my home town of Clairton, PA, a community faced with mountains of discrimination and racism.

Up The Hill – I Have A Dream

On April 4, 1968, Mom sent me on an errand to the corner store just across the street from the Blair Heights housing project where we lived. I skipped back through the concrete courtyards trying to hurry before darkness fell. But on my way back, I heard people screaming, and all the lights were out. I was petrified.

I climbed the three stories, feeling my way in the dark to apartment 7-H and burst through the doors to tell my parents what was going on outside. A rare sight shocked me into silence. My mother sat all balled up on my Dad's lap and both of them were crying. Martin Luther King had been assassinated.

Six months later, we moved out of the projects and purchased our first home. But if we thought leaving Blair Heights meant leaving our sorrows behind, we were wrong.

Our new neighborhood "up the hill" (farther from the steel mills), was friendly enough, but possessed a subtle air of discrimination. Over time, relations between people became quite turbulent as racial riots filled the streets. Our walk to school was lined with police dogs, patrol cars and paddy wagons. Walking was part of the issue. There were no school buses for Black neighborhoods. How befitting that old Motown tunes like "Ain't No Mountain High Enough" blared from Mom's radio.

During my senior year of high school as I sulked about being the sole Black on the Clairton Honey Bears majorette squad and excluded from the private practices, Dad drove to the post office every day to see if I had received an acceptance letter for college. It was his dream.

Look To The Hills

In our family, if parents were having trouble getting along or children were being disobedient, they would have to visit Grandma Hearing's "situation room." As all the relatives were socializing in the living room, Grandma would single out the troubled party. If she said to you softly, "Let's have a talk," that was your cue to get up and follow her painfully slow footsteps through the draped doorway into a hallway that led to her bedroom.

> In troubled times, Grandma always looked to the hills.

Grandma had a quiet strength. She was so smooth, and her words of wisdom would sink in so slowly that most times you wouldn't realize until hours later that you had been set straight. Plus, Grandma's words were always easier to swallow with a taste of her homemade cakes and pies. If only Grandma's techniques could have been used to settle Clairton's racial issues! In troubled times, Grandma always looked to the hills. And more and more, she could be heard calling on her favorite Scripture: "I will lift up mine eyes unto the hills from whence cometh my help" (Ps.121:1).

Endless Mountains

In northeast Pennsylvania, there is a place the Indians once called Endless Mountains. Before the state existed, the area was home to Native Americans. I asked my grandmother, "Why are there pictures of Indian women hanging on your bedroom wall?" She said those were her and granddad's mothers, my great grandmothers. Puzzled, I asked, "But I thought we were Black?" Patiently, she explained our diverse heritage.

Endless Mountains seemed appropriate. The mountainous terrain mirrored the mountains in my life. My first semester at the University of Pittsburgh was both exciting and intimidating. I marveled at the tall, historic buildings with halls that echoed into eternity. I met so many people from places I'd never been. I reported to the Cathedral of Learning and was greeted by Associate Dean, Dr. Jack Daniels, who always gave it to you straight.

"The Quiet Storm" he called me, saying I never spoke up in class but aced all his tests. After seeing so many Black students drop out of college after the first year, he summoned me to his office for a quick lesson in Philosophy 101: "This ain't high school; you'll have to get it for yourself. Once you leave this freshman program you'll be fully integrated into the University system and they don't care nothin' about you."

Courage

Dr. Daniels was right; sophomore year at Pitt was very different. There weren't very many people of color, and the classes were huge! I went right back to being intimidated. I did "okay." Against Dad's wishes, I changed my major from pre-med and was glad to be accepted into the School of Health Professions, until the first day of class when I noticed there were only four minority students. By year's end, I comprised the minority. The others transferred out because the blatant prejudice was just too much. Like after class when the professor would laugh and talk with the other students, but whenever I approached, she was suddenly out of time. Or when the students would hold study sessions off campus at the sorority house and I wasn't invited. It took a lot of courage to stay. I cried a lot.

Where was Dr. Daniels when I needed him?

My mind drifted back to the old Motown tunes on Mom's radio. My head was bobbing along to Diana Ross cooing the lyrics to her anthem "Ain't No Mountain High Enough." But something happened. Suddenly the song penetrated my spirit. Strangely Miss Ross's voice quickly faded and the voice of the Lord emerged, urging me, "If you need me, just call MY NAME." By the end of the song I was sure He was saying, "Fear not. No wind, rain, valley, or mountain could ever keep me from getting to *you!*"

He is there wherever we are on our journey.

Move That Mountain!

We sometimes think God must not want us to have certain blessings because He doesn't perform an instantaneous miracle and bring it to pass. But here's why:

> *"And it came to pass, when Pharaoh had let the people go, that God led them not through the way of the land of the Philistines, although that was near; for God said, lest peradventure the people repent when they see war, and they return to Egypt. But God led the people about, through the way of the wilderness of the Red Sea"*
>
> (Ex. 13:17, 18).

The quickest, easiest path to the Promised Land was lined with the mightiest army of the land. The Israelites were still slaves in their own minds. God said at the very sight of their enemies, they would turn back! *They were not yet strong enough to fight for their blessings. Are you?* We must remember that salvation is free, but promises we have to fight for.

The time spent in the wilderness was necessary to strengthen their faith, to transform them. After their journey, they were able to believe God, overtake their enemies, and pursue their promise!

What should you do with that mountain in your life? Jesus said we should take authority over it and command it to move:

> *"... if you have faith as small as a mustard seed, you can say to this mountain, "Move from here to there," and it will move. Nothing will be impossible for you."*
>
> (Matt.: 17:20, NIV)

God will not do for you what He has already empowered you to do. *Speak to the mountain!* What can we learn from every miracle in the Bible? Your miracle is attached to your obedience. The process you are going through will strengthen you so that you will be able to take hold of your blessing, hang on to it, and not turn back. The next time you encounter that enemy, that debt, that challenge, you will have the wisdom and strength to pursue and overtake it. No enemy will keep you from your promised land.

> God will not do for you what He has already empowered you to do. Speak to the mountain!

Give Me This Mountain

> *"Now therefore, give me this mountain, whereof the Lord spake in that day; for thou heardest in that day how the Anakims were there, and that the cities were great and fenced: if so be the Lord will be with me, then I shall be able to drive them out, as the Lord said."*
>
> (Josh. 14:12)

The children of Israel didn't miss the Promised Land just because they were afraid, but because they allowed their fear to turn to disbelief and eventually to disobedience. They refused to go forward and possess the land. On the other hand, Caleb said to Joshua, I know there are giants in the land that the Lord promised to me, and further more I know that I am old. But I am strong and well able to fight. Now "Give me this mountain!"

Give me this mountain; this business, this ministry, this family, this land, means:

> *I'm ready for the responsibilities.*
> *I'm willing to fight to get it.*
> *I'm willing to fight to keep it.*

God gives us gifts, for the Bible says gifts come without repentance. But promises we must fight for. Having no fear, we can say like Caleb said, "Give me this mountain." Knowing it to be full of enemies of every kind, Caleb was in effect saying, "Bring it on!" He was focused on receiving the promise, even if it meant he had to fight for it.

I chose to fight.

Persistence

Hope showed up my senior year. Like the children of Israel, I had begun to see myself as a grasshopper in a land of giants who were all more qualified than me. Would I shrink back or forge ahead to success? I decided to persist. One day, the professor introduced a graduate student to the class who would be a resource to us as we worked on our senior thesis. He was laid back, smart, and non-biased. He looked over my research and in one session, gave me all the direction I'd been seeking. Now all that was necessary was to complete my final internship at the VA Hospital. The hospital director's feedback would make or break my grade. But it was under her tutelage that I not only had a chance to test what I had learned in the real world, but realized something—I knew this stuff! She sent glowing remarks back to the university, complementing not only my technical knowledge but my interaction with her diverse staff. So there.

I was still receiving the same shabby treatment from my classmates and professors. But I persevered, often hearing Dad's voice: "One thing about education, once you have it, no one can take it away from you."

Finishing My Course

The School of Health Professions graduation ceremony was held on campus at Soldiers and Sailors Memorial Hall, the place the legendary Kathryn Kulhman used to rock with her miracle healing services. How appropriate, I knew I was only there by some miracle.

I didn't make a big fuss about the ceremony to my family, knowing this wasn't the Medical School degree they'd hoped for. Afterward, while the other students were embracing and visiting with friends and family, I started to walk off when I noticed a tall dark man wearing a handsome suit off in the distance. I gasped, then went running.

"Dad!"

He told me he was proud of me and took me to lunch, presenting me to the owner of the restaurant as his daughter that just graduated from Pitt. No, it wasn't Med School, but he was just as proud.

I made it!

> "I have fought a good fight, I have finished my course, I have kept the faith."
>
> (2 Tim. 4:7)

The High Place

> "Every valley shall be exalted, and every mountain and hill shall be made low: and the crooked shall be made straight, and the rough places plain:"
>
> (Isa. 40:4)

As a gospel singer, my early role models were Tramaine Hawkins and Sara Jordan-Powell. Through Sara's recordings she mentored me on how to open up my range with power. It seemed everywhere I went I was requested to sing "The High Place."

> *I will make the darkness light before you*
> *What is wrong I'll make it right before you*

*All thy battles I will fight before you
And the high place I'll bring down*

Years later, I met Sara at a conference where she prayed for me. She said, "So when you think no one is praying, remember Sara is praying for you." She has such a sweet spirit, you almost miss the power. But walking away, I realized with each step that a heavy anointing was flowing through me and that, through prayer, I had received an impartation!

Singing "The High Place" over and over was very befitting. It reminded me that all the mountains in my life were no match for the power of God.

Are there mountains in your life? Do you find yourself saying "if only" this, I might have done that? You've got to keep on going. *Tell that mountain to move and know that nothing shall be impossible to you!*

> Tell that mountain to move and know that nothing shall be impossible to you!

Reflections Of The Journey

- Even in the best seasons of your life, you will face adversity or something that blocks access to your dream.

- A mountain is something that has exalted itself in your life, and is standing between you and your promise.

- What should you do with that mountain in your life? Jesus said we should take authority over it and command it to move.

- Salvation is free, but promises we must fight for.

- God will not do for you what He has already empowered you to do.

- Your miracle is attached to your obedience.

- Speak to the mountain!

The Journey Continues . . .

Chapter 6
Through The Valley

If mountains are about things you are trying to get to, valleys are about things you need to leave behind. Valley experiences are *the lowest points in life*, not just stumbling over a ditch, but a *deep depression*. Caution: As you read on you will feel the descent into the deep, dark places of the valley. Grief can be quite intoxicating, pulling you in deeper and deeper. But remember, your job is to go through the valley, not to dwell therein.

Shadows Of Death

On starry nights, Dad would sit me on his knee on the back porch and have me wish upon a star. Then he'd tell me stories of his worldwide travels in the U.S. Navy. Some ports he'd describe so vividly I felt I was sailing right along with him. There we'd sit, stargazing for hours. He truly put me in awe of the constellations. Then out of the silence, Dad's rich baritone voice would bellow old Navy tunes. And oh, how I'd laugh at the Louis Armstrong facial expressions he'd make while singing "What a Wonderful World."

> Valley experiences are the lowest points in life, not just stumbling over a ditch, but a deep depression.

A year out of college, I had made plans to leave home and rent a town home with friends in Pittsburgh, an hour away from my family and much closer to my job. But Mom and Dad had a proposition of their own: a car, new bedroom furniture, and new clothes. They really wanted me to stay at home. So I did.

Not long after, Dad's health began to fail. A nagging cough developed into a diagnosis of lung cancer, which rapidly took its toll on his fifty-seven-year-old body. "I lived like a man, and I'll die like a man," he'd say. Eventually he'd give in, and put his head on my shoulder. When I'd come home in the evenings, I'd know he was still awake by the glowing embers from his cigarette. He would bend his arm upward at the elbow, meaning for me to come hold his hand. One snowy night, I decided to stay in Pittsburgh instead of risking the drive through bad weather, not knowing that the next morning Dad would suffer seizures and be rushed to the hospital. I met my brother Ted and sister-in-law Jacquie there and we had a private consultation with the doctor. It was brief: "Make funeral arrangements." But as he was speaking, I was thinking, *Not today, not on my watch!*

Voice From Beyond

I stood over my father's bed, weeping and apologizing for not being home the night before. The doctor came up behind me. "He can't hear you. He's in an irreversible comatose state. By the way, do you think he would want you to consent to a Do Not Resuscitate order?" Just then the bed began to shake and Dad's eyes began to roll up toward the ceiling. "He can hear us!" I cried. "He knows we're talking about letting him go!" I was inconsolable.

The doctor sympathized and left me alone to talk to my dad, and to my heavenly Father, asking for another chance to bring Dad home. Every day I sat, sang, and prayed, until Dad very mysteriously, but clearly said, "I wanna give up the ghost, honey." The ICU nurse looked on in amazement. He was out of the coma! He clearly wanted to die, but I convinced him to come home once more. The next day they moved him to a recovery room where we had the strangest conversation:

"Oh, Dad, I'm so glad to see you. You really scared me! And look at you, sitting up and eating. I'm so proud of you!"

"Yeah, but there's too many people."

"You mean there are more nurses and patients on this floor?"

"No, I'm talking about all the people coming to see me."

"Oh, you had visitors? Well, I'll just tell the nurse not to let anyone…"

"Didn't you see all those cars when you came in?"

"Well of course, Dad. We're at a hospital."

"No, honey… I'm dead."

Silence. (Breathe, Stacie. Just breathe).

Was he describing his funeral? He was rubbing his chin, looking out somewhere beyond where we were. Yes, I had called him back to this life, but he had already entered the shadows of death. Now he was confused.

"Dad, look at me." Eventually he did. "Do you see me?" He looked bewildered, but nodded, yes. I held his hand. "Do you feel me?" He nodded again. "Am I dead too?"

He thought, then said, "No, honey."

I said, "If I'm alive and you're here with me, you must still be alive too, right?"

He agreed. I tried to swallow, but couldn't. I became aware of how loud my heart was beating. Ka, thump. Ka thump. Ka thump.

RIIINNNNGG!

The phone made me jump, snapping me out of my worry. It was Dad's brother saying he was coming soon. I felt refreshed and even strong enough to let Dad finish telling me about his funeral.

Several days and many visits to Dad's bedside passed. Then one day at work, I returned a call to the hospital. "What? But how? He's completely bedridden, can't feed or change himself… Who will? But they insisted. Driving to the hospital that evening, the Lord reminded me, *You asked me to bring him home again.*

Sitting next to Dad's bed, I could hear the nurse speaking but it was as though she was speaking in slow motion. "As soon as he arrives home give him the green pills three times a day for four days, then decrease the dosage (*What?*). Start the white pills and crush them in baby food" (*Huh?*).

"I am not a nurse," I said. "What if I give him the wrong dosage on the wrong day?" The more she talked, the heavier my shoulders felt. "And before we release him, you'll have to demonstrate that you can change his catheter. (*What! Oh, dear God, help me!*). She saw the tears and stopped talking to console me. "Honey, don't you have anyone to help you?"

"It…it'll be all right," I said, more to convince myself than her. "It'll be all right."

I cleaned the room next to mine and put fresh linens on the Craft-matic bed. The next morning I stood on the staircase overlooking the foyer as they rolled him in.

"Stacie! Why did you send for me?" he called. I had to laugh and started to tell him, I most certainly did not. But then remembered, I most certainly did. Through prayer, I had called him back from the valley of the shadow of death.

The Anointing For My Assignment

As snow fell outside the window by Dad's bed, I sat nervously with the nurse's instructions in my hand. That evening, Grandma Gaynor called and prayed. But I couldn't sleep, listening from the next room for Dad's every breath, wondering if he had pulled the oxygen tubes out of his nose again. Finally, I slept in a chair in his room.

Suddenly I awakened, it was morning. I sprang to my feet knowing exactly what to do. In my sleep, I had a vision of three pages posted on a mirror. So, I posted the charts on the mirror, filling in what Dad was to have, by day and time. I cleaned him, fed him, and medicated him on that schedule.

> *"In a dream, in a vision of the night, when deep sleep falleth upon men, in slumberings upon the bed; Then He openeth the ears of men, and sealeth their instruction,"*
>
> (Job 33:15-16)

In my sleep, God gave me the anointing for my assignment. That must have been what Grandma prayed! I learned then that *an anointing is available for whatever God assigns to you.* By the time Grandma arrived, I was a completely different person. All she said was, "My, my, my."

> An anointing is available for whatever God assigns to you.

Like John the Baptist, Grandma Gaynor was known for her sharp tongue and fiery prophetic utterances. She'd carry a bullhorn into the housing projects and cry out, "Repent, every one of you!" We'd hear all about it the next day at school. But at Dad's bedside, she softly entertained me with faith-filled stories of the many times God miraculously healed her. At Dad's bedside, she leaned over and whispered to him, "Ted, that baby you used to hold is now holding you."

No Tears In Heaven

The family convinced me to take a break and return to work. But about an hour into the workday, they started calling me. Dad was refusing medication and asking for the nurse (that would be me). And he was insisting that he had an appointment at 2:00 p.m. I made my way back to our hometown, but not in time to say good-bye. That gave me thoughts of intense guilt. Surely Dad thought I had given up on him by leaving that morning. But then my sister-in-law said the last thing Dad did was to bend his arm upward at the elbow, raising his hand. When she took it, he kissed her hand good-bye, believing it to be mine. It was around 2:00 pm.

I handled the funeral arrangements, and even sang. But something was strange. I confessed to Grandma Gaynor that I couldn't cry. I thought it was because I was too busy taking care of everything and trying to be strong for everyone else. But surprisingly, she whispered, "Me either." She said God was keeping us strong for something He could see down the road that we couldn't.

When Dreams Die

Mom was in pain, and we all felt it because we had all lived through it. I asked the Lord what it was all about. He said it was where I learned to love unconditionally, to love people most when they deserve it least.

London Tailoring

A former Sunday school teacher, Mom taught us our first hymns and said our prayers with us each night. She'd also joke around with us, making quite a fuss until Dad would yell, "Sam, you kids cut it out!" (as if she were one of the kids too). But Mom was happiest when she was working. She was the first black woman to own a business in Clairton's business district, a dry cleaners called London Tailoring. She and Dad worked hard to obtain the dream of home ownership. But shortly after purchasing the two-story brick home with a cellar and finished attic, Mom lost London Tailoring due to a bad business decision, for which she partially faulted Dad.

She would never be the same.

The Secret Inside

We suffered two devastating fires in the house on Halcomb Avenue (bad wiring, they said). Those were the days of Spam, sardines, beans and rice, and stretching ground meat with stale bread crumbs. It was the sacrifice we made to live in a house that we couldn't even afford to heat. It made us miss the projects, like the children of Israel longing for Egypt, where heat was free.

Mom became severely depressed and escaped for periods of time through alcohol. It was like we had two mothers. One was beautiful and nurturing, with a spotless house and always a hot pot of homemade something on the stove. But we kept the other mom a secret, locked inside our tidy new house, forbidden to speak about it outside the family.

Losing London Tailoring was like losing her soul. The depression Mom suffered grew more severe over time. After Dad passed, I decided to intervene.

Although she resisted me, I checked Mom into a hospital, hoping to get her into treatment. But before I knew it, she was back home, and things only worsened. One day I found her seizing on the kitchen floor. My days were filled with worry and frustration, like I was screaming in a dream. And I was so, so tired. Late one night I fell asleep at the wheel on River Road. By a miracle, I avoided all the oncoming vehicles and hit the guardrail clear on the other side of the road. The daily commute to Pittsburgh and back had finally taken its toll.

Love and Happiness

It was a hard decision, but just before the holidays, my brother moved me to my first apartment. I took Mom to see my new place and my brother's. She said she was proud of us.

> *Merry Christmas Stacie,*
>
> *I want you to know that I love you very much and miss you twice as much, but of course I wish you love and happiness for the rest of your life. Thanks loads for being there when I needed you...*
>
> *Merry Christmas*
> *With Love*
> *Mom*

"Love and happiness" was not just what she wished for me, but what she had searched for all her life. Just a few short months later, my sweet mother mysteriously slipped away.

I just couldn't believe I'd lost her so young and only a year after Dad. I needed to know why. So I was angry when the family doctor released her body with no autopsy. Now I would never know. A nurse friend explained that the doctor was probably trying to protect me in his actions. If the autopsy revealed any evidence of suicide, life insurance benefits would be denied.

Suicide? What was she thinking? That I had abandoned her? That I considered her a burden? My questions would never be answered. But this much I do know: she died with the pain inside. Worse, she died with her dreams locked inside, like a beautiful, unopened gift.

Close Encounters Of The Ungodly Kind

Church was all I had left. After college graduation, it became my second home. I especially enjoyed the revivals when guest preachers came from all over, and people got saved and healed. Some people you hadn't seen since the last revival would come and get saved and healed—again.

But enemies were everywhere. I make mention of the following incidents only to stress this point: *When the enemy has an assignment on your life, he'll use anyone, anywhere to take you out. Stay vigilant and alert!* And stay on course.

One bitter winter night after a revival service, we all grabbed a bite to eat. Afterward, the guest preacher realized that he and I were parked in the same parking lot. He saw me safely to my car then briskly walked to his. I was still warming up my car when a knock on the window startled me. I was relieved to see that it was him, until I rolled the window down and within seconds he plunged his tongue down my throat and his hand down my blouse. "Drive safely," he said as he sauntered away. A gust of icy wind made me realize my window was still down and my hands were frozen to the steering wheel. I sat staring in the cold until a tear rolled down my cheek. Church had been my last sanctuary, now the enemy had taken that too. I knew my pastor would have been furious with his respected colleague, had I told him about the assault. Instead, I responded by blaming myself and becoming more withdrawn and less trusting about who I let into my personal space.

However, nothing could have prepared me for what happened next. A friend of the church was on his death bed. We all visited his home in shifts until his family arrived from out of town. During my visit, the other person on my shift ran to the store. Suddenly, the "dead" came back to life, mustering enough strength to grab at me for one last thrill. I pushed him away and ran out of there like I'd seen a ghost! About a week later, as I was entertaining guests at home, the dying man showed up at my door. He begged my forgiveness, kissed my forehead, and left. He went home and died that night.

The Enemy's Plot Revealed

I can't say this loudly enough: Thank God I had encountered many true godly men and fathers in the gospel along my path prior to those unpleasant experiences. Otherwise, I might have been derailed from my journey. If you are among those who have turned their backs on religion because of the actions of a careless Christian, please don't judge God based on the deeds of men! *The enemy knows you can't grow into your destiny with the root of bitterness inside of you.*

> The enemy knows you can't grow into your destiny with the root of bitterness inside of you.

That is, after, all what the enemy was plotting against me. He wanted to discourage me from growing along the path God had set before me. The battle that had begun in my childhood was still on, only the faces changed. Now that the devil's plot was exposed, I became more determined, if not curious. What was it about me that made him so nervous that he assigned an enemy to every step of my path from birth?

What trauma or tragic circumstances are going on in your life? Most valleys are due to loss. You may have been stripped of something valuable to you—your health, a home, or business. Maybe you're mourning the death of a loved one, or a failed marriage. I'm sure it's not what you would have expected or planned. How do you even begin to rise?

The Scripture gives a clue: "Yea, though I *walk through* …"

Yes, in your valley you will rest beside quiet streams, and the Good Shepherd will refresh and restore your soul. But then you must get up! Don't get stuck there. In the valley, the only way out is "through." So keep walking with determination and declare:

> *"Yea, though I walk through the valley of the shadow of death, I shall fear no evil…"*
>
> (Ps. 23:4)

> In the valley, the only way out is "through."

And Miles To Go ...

At McKeesport Cemetery I knelt at Dad's grave on the hillside in the veterans section, not quite knowing what to say. Then finally managed to whisper, "Dad, Mom's here too." I felt like I was telling on myself, as if I had failed. I sat weeping in that cold cemetery. I wanted to crawl inside one of the graves. Then I remembered a Robert Frost poem Dad used to quote to me:

> *The woods are lovely, dark and deep*
> *But I have promises to keep*
> *And miles to go before I sleep*
> *And miles to go before I sleep.*

Now I understood that he was telling me to go on. *It was not my time to sleep.* But by the time I reached Mom's gravesite in the civilian section, I had emotionally flat-lined. I was frozen inside, although my body was heaving with tears. All the crying I couldn't do before started in that graveyard. For two or three years after, I woke up crying, drove to work crying, and had to leave my desk several times a day. I swallowed food with tears. Little by little, I plunged into a dark place that no one could reach. It is painful to cry dry tears. My parents' love was locked inside me. My belly literally swelled with pain. I was tormented by nightmares and thoughts of *Why couldn't I save them? Why wasn't I there in their last hour?* I was diagnosed with a spasmodic, digestive disorder, and was prescribed tranquilizers. I was in a daze. I felt like I was rifling through my purse thinking, *Hmmm, now where did I put my sanity?*

A valley is a deep depression in the earth. Our valley experiences are also depressions. I didn't realize then that's what I was going through. Back then, it wasn't *tres chic* to see a therapist. One painful night, I lay on the sofa of my Squirrel Hill apartment and told God I wasn't waking up tomorrow. In my heart, I said good-bye to my loved ones. The next morning when I awakened, I was angry with God. How could He leave me all alone in this world? For the first time in my life, I didn't talk to

Him, didn't pray. The enemy saw the open door, seized the opportunity, and sent people into my life to help pull me away.

Have you ever felt your heart slipping into darkness, but were too numb to care?

Peace In The Valley

The one thing I did right was to stay in the house of God. Eventually the Word reached me and God's love brought me back. When I finally lifted my head, I saw His hand and grabbed on tight. He held me as if to say, "I missed you!" Whenever I hear CeCe Winans belt out "Mercy Said No," I think back to those times and am so, so thankful that *mercy will never let me slip away.*

I'm thankful because I found that *the best cure for grief is gratitude.* Being thankful for all you once had, for what still remains, and what lies ahead.

I fell on my knees like I was falling into His arms. For the first time in a long time, my own ears heard my lips whisper "thank you," softly and repeatedly. Soon it built into a crescendo. Thank you. Thank you! Suddenly I felt life pumping back into me, and I experienced something so glorious. He flooded my heart with an overwhelming peace and a supernatural joy. What a beautiful picture I still have of me with hands lifted and fresh tears glistening on my face. I never thought I'd feel that way again, I was alive! It can happen to you too. When it happened to me, I vowed to never let it go. Never would I let anyone or anything take it away from me. I packed my bag with that one thing inside, the only that mattered to me: *"The peace that passes all understanding"* (Phil. 4:7). And I began to make my ascent from the valley.

But I Have Promises To Keep ...

The land begins to incline as you exit the valley. But what you once valued has been replaced with grief, heartache, worry and shame. With each step your shoulders have slumped lower beneath the weight of sorrow, bitterness, and guilt. So you have a choice. In order to maneuver the slopes, you must *lay aside every weight and every burden, both yours and* other people's. Lay aside sin, sickness, mistakes, and unforgiveness. As you begin your ascent, you can't carry these things with you.

> In the valley, your peace is your power!

Oh, how devastated I was the day the courthouse clerk directed me to the door that read "Orphan's Court" to settle my parent's estate. But *in the valley, your peace is your power!* I found it in the Word of God:

"When my father and my mother forsake me, then the Lord will take me up."

(Ps. 27:10)

"I will not leave you as orphans: I will come to you."

(John 14:18, NIV)

God ... Where Were You?

Looking back on some of the longest, darkest periods of our lives, we sometimes wonder "Where was God?" It took some time, but I began to realize that though I felt forsaken, I was never alone. He hadn't left me, nor given up on me. Only recently did I hear God's answer to my question of His whereabouts during my depressed, lethargic state, with no will to go on. He said that *He was in my future waiting for me to leave my past!*

Of course, there were other questions that would haunt me for the rest of my life: Did Dad think I'd abandoned him, given up on him? And what about Mom, did she also think that I abandoned her? Did she choose to die? *Was it suicide?*

> He was in my future waiting for me to leave my past!

One thing was clear. Our family was under the shadow of death. Year after year, we continued to lose family members. So when death visited me, and tempted me, I was so comfortable with it, I welcomed it. But "Mercy said no." I won't let you go. I won't let you slip away. In the absence of Dad, I sought hard after my heavenly Father. He led me out of the valley of the shadow of death. And even today, when the nightmares return, I pray and they vanish in the wind. He gives me peaceful rest. I emerged from the valley knowing Him to be a healer, a comforter, and a light in darkness.

Reflections Of The Journey

"Five Things You Must Do To Ascend From Your Valley"

1. Keep walking. "The only way out is through."

2. Know that "Your peace is your power!"

3. Lay aside every burden (yours and other people's).

4. Understand that "The best cure for grief is gratitude."

5. Grab on to God's hand and don't let go. He's in your future waiting for you to leave your past!

The Journey Continues . . .

Chapter 7
Purpose In The Pain

Who told you that having faith in God means you'll no longer have troubles in life? What walking with God means is that you will never walk alone, because He has promised never to forsake you. And it means that everything that happens in your life (good or bad) will somehow work together for your good.

One crisp October morning, after my move to Austin, Texas, music awakened me and I reached for the snooze. A song was playing and I just couldn't get the radio to turn off. I finally just got out of bed. That's when I realized it was Saturday, and I hadn't set the alarm. The song I heard wasn't on the radio, it was in my dreams:

> *Can I please walk beside you, Can I lead and guide you,*
>
> *Can I walk with you and talk with you, My Dear.*
>
> *Can I please console you, understand and know you,*
>
> *Can I hold you close when you need it most, My Dear.*

Can I please take your hand, Can I help you to stand,
Can I be your light all through the night, My Dear.

I did not realize what the Lord was saying to me until about a month later when again I awakened, but this time with a dull pain in my lower abdomen. I got dressed for work, but kept needing to sit down. At the office, a coworker handed me a half a roll of Tums, "It's just gas, Hon. I get that all the time." But I knew something was wrong and ambled across the atrium to the medical unit. The nurses immediately rushed me to the hospital, with two co-workers following behind in a car. As I was escorted behind the ER doors, I glanced back as if to say, "Be right back. We'll do lunch."

But later that evening, following test after test, I was still being poked, prodded and probed in every way possible. I began to hyperventilate and blacked out. When I came around, I had oxygen tubes in my nose and an IV in my arm, with more drama to come. They had decided to catheterize me for a pelvic ultrasound. Ugh! I was exhausted and in pain. Finally I began to cry. The poker faces on the two ultrasound technicians led me to believe nothing was there. But the doctor gave the news: a large mass in my pelvis. An ovarian tumor.

The next morning as the nurse weighed me in, I gasped at how much weight I had lost. I quickly dropped more pounds by the week. I was so appalled at my image, I taped Scriptures over the mirror so I wouldn't see myself.

Knocking On Heaven's Door

Cancer. At least according to all the test results. But surgery was the only way to confirm. Nothing the doctor tried worked to rid my body of the tumor, or to ease my discomfort. Sleep escaped me and my body rejected all food and medicine. The pain was so intense I had to crawl to the bathroom. That's when the song came back to me, *Can I please take your hand, can I help you to stand, My Dear?* If I dozed off, the pain would jerk me back awake. *Can I be your light all through the night, My Dear?*

The doctor decided to schedule surgery right away, but agreed to hold off until after Thanksgiving. I wanted to see Sister. I thought it might be the last time. Then I wanted to go home – as in heavenly home.

Meanwhile, I found that holding a hot gel pack on my abdomen gave me some relief. So I made an effort to return to work, but my co-workers quickly escorted me back out to the parking lot. (Sigh) Sitting at a stop light, I turned on Austin's only gospel station and learned there was a revival in town that night. Before my next thought, I felt impressed by the Lord to attend service that night and (oddly) to give an offering. Before service, I searched for the Scripture Grandma would quote over me as a child while anointing my tongue with oil, but I couldn't find it.

I wrapped myself up in my little black shawl and sat in the back of the meeting room. "Woman in the black, stand, if you're able," I heard the preacher say. Just before he prayed for me he quoted the very Scripture I had been looking for: "I am the Lord that healeth thee." When I returned home, my Bible was *laying open* to the book of Exodus, "I am the Lord that healeth thee!" I thought, *Hmmm, maybe the Lord wants to heal me*.

Heaven Can Wait

I sort of said, "Thanks Lord, but no thanks." I wasn't afraid to die, knowing that as a born-again Christian, when I take my last breath on Earth, my very next breath would be in the glorious presence of Jesus. He would be glad to see me, welcome me home and say, "Well done!" I dozed off to sleep, but once again was jerked awake. Only I realized it wasn't pain that awakened me so suddenly. It was a question lingering the air:

"Have you done what I sent you to do?"

Huh? "Sent" me to do?

I thought about the question for a long time. I didn't know the answer. I never knew I was sent to do anything. Now I wasn't happy about going to heaven anymore. There was a heaviness. I asked, half in anger, "Lord, for what reason are you keeping me here?"

Well, when the student is ready, the teacher will appear.

> Have you done what I sent you to do?

That teacher was Dr. Myles Munroe. Back then, there was no "Purpose Driven Life." No one else had a clue what I was talking about. I felt alone and confused as to whether I had really heard God speaking. *Was I the only human being that didn't know there was a purpose to my existence?*

While watching TBN, I heard a man with a Bahamian accent teaching about purpose. I lit up like Fourth of July fireworks! My face was inches away from the TV screen as I began to take it all in. It was like the day Abraham met Melchizedek. Finally, someone had heard what I heard from God! I began watching Dr. Munroe's program regularly and was astonished at his revelation on purpose. Why hadn't I heard this stuff before? It gave me hope and a reason to live.

Heaven can wait!

Through my pain, God revealed purpose to me. Until then, I believed I was a mistake (since my parents had not planned for me). Now I knew that God had planned for me and chosen me to be in Him before the world was ever made (Eph. 1:4). In fact, He chose the precise time I would be born into.

"Oprah, what's your greatest fear?" Larry King asked.

"Not using all of my potential," she replied.

My greatest fear is similar—not fulfilling God's plan for my life.

It is my soul's desire.

Healing Hands

I decided to live. I had to. *I did not want to be known eternally in Heaven as one who did not complete her destiny.* So God and I had a brief chat:

"Lord, this is big."

"I'm bigger."

"Let's do this."

After all, I had fought for my life all of my life. Why give up now?

I pasted yet another Scripture on my mirror: "I shall not die, but live, and declare the works of the Lord" (Ps. 118:17). I tried hard to believe that, but all of my symptoms were still there. My body still appeared to be dying. So I taped up another Scripture: "Therefore we do not lose heart. Even though our outward man is wasting away, yet the inward man is being renewed day by day" (2 Cor. 4:16).

On Thanksgiving Day, Sister picked me up at Houston Hobby airport. When I came creeping toward her wrapped in my little black shawl, I fell into her arms with teary eyes, and in a weak raspy breath uttered, "Sister". She tried not to show her shock, but later admitted she was quite alarmed by my appearance. On the drive to her house, I gave the doctor's report. She placed me in an upstairs bedroom while she finished up Thanksgiving dinner for her guests. I told her not to worry about me, but agreed to take some herbal supplements just to appease her. She came back with soup, even though I wasn't able to keep anything down. But an amazing thing happened. When she returned about two hours later, I had slept, and licked the bowl of soup clean! I asked groggily, "What did you give me?" As she explained the herbal remedies for each of my symptoms, I flashed back to our childhood when she was always concocting something. Who knew this gift that had been evident in her youth would turn around and save my life?

It was Thanksgiving. And I was thankful.

My Path To Healing

On the way back to the airport, I was taking notes while Sister drove and schooled me on what supplements to pick up from Whole Foods. It was the first stop I made when I got back to Austin. I would sit and read books on nutrition and natural healing for hours at Whole Foods as the Lord continued to give me instructions. I had hope.

I had also heard Dodie Osteen's testimony of quoting healing Scriptures three times a day like medicine, and followed her example.

Just before surgery, the doctor ordered another ultrasound. Amazingly, I had the same two technicians that performed the original test. They remembered me, and I remembered their stony faces when they would not reveal the test results. But not this time. They both screamed when the image came up on the screen, then swiveled the monitor around so I could see it too– or not see it. The tumor was gone! The surgery was cancelled!

Look at God. *He stepped between me and death—again.*

Purpose In The Pain

Wait… if you blinked you missed it!

It was when the enemy launched his greatest attack that I surrendered my whole life to God (past, present and future). Right there, wounded on the battlefield and under heavy fire, was where the Lord reached me and breathed purpose into my life. It was the moment that forever changed my course.

There was purpose in the pain! All things did work together for my good!

Not long after I began watching Dr. Munroe's program, I was relocated back to Houston and was praying about a church home. Now that I had stepped into purpose, I needed something to take me to the next level of my spiritual journey. I saw a pastor on a local Christian TV network and seemed drawn to this ministry. The day I walked in the doors of the church, Pastor Smith "so happened" to be teaching a series about purpose. I joined! The phenomenal gift in that pastor drew out the gift in me that empowered me to rise up, begin to speak the Word to my world, and "flow in purpose."

> You may not have chosen these times, but these times have chosen you.

Now let me empower you. You may not have chosen these times, but these times have chosen you.

The more my eyes began to open, the more thankful I was that the Lord's plans prevailed and not mine. Had I missed this time, I would have missed my destiny.

To Him That Endureth

I survived.

Because of the abuse I suffered during childhood at the hands of the multitudes, crowds were never my favorite place to be. I much prefer working behind the scenes, but God's ways are not our ways. His plans are higher than ours. I am also convinced that He has a sense of humor, especially when I saw unexpected events unfold—like being appointed as a major corporation's media spokesperson for the fourth largest city in the country. Or that I would coordinate the company's presence in major community events drawing crowds from 200 to 200,000 – and enjoying it! Or that I would write and record songs for all to hear. All this from a little girl who hid in closets and was too afraid to speak? (No wonder Grandma used to anoint my tongue with oil.)

God doesn't just offer a survival plan; He offers the promise of abundant life. It was as if to say: The baby that wasn't planned for, that was too weak to live and breathe on her own, that wasn't strong enough to fight her enemies, the same shall live again, rise up, and do exploits.

I learned this:

> *"For we wrestle not against flesh and blood, but against principalities, against powers, against the rulers of the darkness of this world, against spiritual wickedness in high places."*
>
> (Eph. 6:12)

In other words, the real fight is in the spirit! We all wrestle against the powers of darkness.

Look back over your life. *Are you aware of the assignment the enemy has had on your life, perhaps since birth?* Sickness, abuse, lack? Anything to take you out! I learned to put on the whole armor of God and be strong in the Lord, because He *always* causes me to triumph in Christ.

God's love reaches beyond survival. He desires that we be "more than conquerors," and overcomers in the faith.

Say to yourself, I will not only survive, but live!

Reflections Of The Journey

- Walking with God means you will never walk alone, and it means that everything that happens in your life (good or bad) will somehow work together for your good.

- Have you done what He "sent" you to do?

- Are you aware of the assignment the enemy has had on your life, perhaps since birth?

- The real fight is in the spirit!

- God's love reaches beyond survival. You are "more than a conqueror," and an overcomer in the faith.

- You may not have chosen these times, but these times have chosen you.

- Say to yourself, "I will not only survive, but live!"

The Journey Continues . . .

> "History is a relentless master. It has no present, only the past rushing to the future. To try to hold fast is to be swept aside."
>
> – John Fitzgerald Kennedy

Chapter 8
Changing Your Course – Growing into Greatness

Yes, you are the "sent" one. Sent with a specific mission and vision to fulfill.

How exciting!

But why does it seem that each time you commit to taking a step forward, another obstacle appears? And if God really wants you to have something, why is it so challenging to obtain it?

Success is a journey. It's not just about an event, but the process. If we yield to the process, it will take us where we want to go. What's different about you now than when you started out on your journey? What did you learn; how did you change?

When God shows us our dream, we expect to see an immediate demonstration. However, *we must grow into greatness.* Success costs something. It is a developmental process that requires change, risk, humility, and sacrifice.

Change does not mean everything you've done in the past is wrong. It may have been good for that time and place in your life. But you're growing now, and in a different place. You cannot rely on past accomplishments for future success.

Your ability to change can be your greatest asset.

The Pride Of Life

There are seven things the Lord hates (Prov. 6:16). Topping the list is pride. All seven are worthy of mention but we will limit our focus to pride for the purpose of this discussion.

It's one thing to say, just as I am, Lord I come to thee. Truly, that's the only way you can come to God—as who you are, right where you are. But it is a dangerous thing to exalt your will above the will of God, to say, this is who I am, this is the way I'm going to stay, to live my life. Can't change, won't change, not even for you, God.

> *"Pride goes before destruction, a haughty spirit before a fall."*
> (Prov. 16:18, NIV)

If you failed at something, look back to reflect on areas where you may have overlooked the opportunity to make necessary changes. You may have even refused to change: refusal to go back to school, seek counseling, change jobs. I never thought of lack of effort to change as pride. But I realized as long as I continued with my old ways of thinking, instead of receiving the mind of Christ on the matter, I was essentially saying my way was better than His.

> *"There is a way which seemeth right unto a man, but the end thereof are the ways of death."*
> (Prov.14:12)

> You cannot rely on past accomplishments for future success.

We often refer to our problems in terms of the pain we are experiencing. But pain is not really the problem; it's a symptom. It's a signal that a problem needs to be addressed. Pain in your body tells you something is wrong. Persistent pain in your life tells you something is out of order. *The pain in your life will persist until you change something you are doing or the way you are thinking.* Stretch beyond the limitations of the human mind and seek the wisdom of God. Whenever I think I've thought of everything, He amazes me by revealing His wisdom on the matter.

His Way Is Perfect

Sometimes we think we have it all figured out. We have strategically planned and organized to the best of our abilities. We sit back and gaze at this wonderful blueprint for success and think, *What a masterpiece!* We look to the Lord, just knowing, anticipating He must be thinking the same and beaming with pride. After all, it is pure perfection! Or is it? Be very sure that your plans line up with His. Yes, the Lord has plans for your life:

> *"For I know the plans I have for you, declares the Lord, plans to prosper you and not to harm you, plans to give you a hope and a future."*
> (Jer. 29:11, NIV)

From where you stand, you may be thinking, What could be better than what I have going right now? Caution: to assure success, seek God's approval and guidance before proceeding.

> *"Commit your actions to the Lord, and your plans will succeed."*
> (Pr. 16:3, NLT)

His ways are far better than ours:

> *"God's way is perfect. All the Lord's promises prove true..."*
> (Ps. 18:30, NLT)

The devil has no creative power. He can only take what God has created and twist it, perverting it into something that fits his agenda. Beautiful music, dance, and poetry, all created by God for His glory, become vile, sexually explicit, twisted and demeaning in the hands of the enemy.

Take a look at your own gifts and talents. Through your eyes, have you limited the ways in which God could use you by imposing your own thoughts and abilities? Has perversion taken over your gift and caused you to exalt darkness and worldliness? Imagine how the world would be if we each allowed the anointing of God to flow through us and use us as He purposed.

Can you imagine?

Because I have sometimes gone my own way in life, I have found myself in some ungodly situations. But my testimony is not that my own way is perfect. My declaration is that His way is perfect, always.

The way God has designed for you may not be profitable for someone else. But for you, it is pure perfection! You have to believe that. You must trust that. God masterminded a divine path for each of our journeys.

> The steps of a good man are ordered by the Lord, and He delights in his way.

Blessed are you who hunger and thirst for the right path.

Blessed are you who seek and find.

In the end, the plan of the Lord will stand:

"The steps of a good man are ordered by the Lord, and He delights in his way."

(Ps. 37:23)

As The Story Goes ...

> *A US navy ship's radio conversation with Canadian authorities off the coast of Newfoundland was released by the Chief of Naval Operations in October, 1995.*
>
> *Americans: "Please divert your course 15 degrees to the North to avoid a collision."*
>
> *Canadians: "Recommend you divert YOUR course 15 degrees to the South to avoid a collision."*

Americans: "This is the captain of a US Navy ship. I say again, divert YOUR course."

Canadians: "NO, I say again, you divert YOUR course."

Americans: "THIS IS THE AIRCRAFT CARRIER USS ABRAHAM LINCOLN, THE SECOND LARGEST SHIP IN THE UNITED STATES' ATLANTIC FLEET. WE ARE ACCOMPANIED BY THREE DESTROYERS, THREE CRUISERS AND NUMEROUS SUPPORT VESSELS. I DEMAND THAT YOU CHANGE YOUR COURSE 15 DEGREES NORTH. THAT'S ONE-FIVE DEGREES NORTH, OR COUNTER MEASURES WILL BE UNDERTAKEN TO ENSURE THE SAFETY OF THIS SHIP."

Canadians: "This is a lighthouse. Your call."

Friend, as good as your plans may be, it would be most wise to change your course and align your will with Almighty God than to demand that He change His.

"For I am the Lord, I change not;"

(Mal. 3:6)

Think of your thought process as the mammoth USS aircraft; old and established. It takes some time to turn it around. Don't wait until you come face to face with a crisis. Start now to avoid tragic results. Awareness of upcoming change is critical.

Before Honor Is Humility

"A man's pride shall bring him low: but honor shall uphold the humble in spirit."

(Prov.29:23)

Dad used to say to me as a kid, "Don't let nobody give you no wooden nickels" (something he

> A man's pride shall bring him low: but honor shall uphold the humble in spirit.

learned in the military). It was symbolic for not letting anyone get over on you in life.

Fresh out of college and holding down my first real job, a retired army sergeant had just come on board. He was used to giving orders and getting his way. And he was loud. From the second story of our office building we could hear him entering on the first floor. He was known to bark out orders to coworkers, reducing many to tears. My turn would come.

Everyone else I worked with was aware of my Christian values, and even respected them. But "Sarge" ridiculed me daily. One day he jumped from his seat, put his finger in my face, and yelled to the top of his voice. "You Bible-toting, uppity, self-righteous, holier than thou, etc...." A boldness came over me. I quoted a Scripture and kept on walking. This infuriated him and he stormed out of the building. Only when everyone was certain he was gone did they burst into laughter. They said of all people, they couldn't believe I didn't cry.

Not long after, a supervisory position came open. We both put in for it. He went to the Director's office and tried to pull rank. He acknowledged that I had been there a little longer, but on the other hand, he had many years of experience as a military officer. He was so confident in getting the job, he actually moved into the Supervisor's office across the hall with the big window. He had to move right back though, when it was announced that the position was mine.

But the office with the view wasn't for me either. About that same time, I was offered a much higher paying job across town with a company car and expense account. On my last day, in front of everyone, he laughed about how I had stood up to him. And, he gave me a wooden nickel!

Feelings *(Whoa, Whoa, Whoa, Feelings)*

Feelings are real. Feelings are powerful. But feelings are not always your friend! *Feelings will tell you that right is wrong, and absolutely convince you that wrong is right.*

It is argued that you can't help who you fall in love with. So what if it happens to be your married boss. An anorexic *feels* she is still grossly overweight. A pedophile *feels* uncontrollable sexual desires toward children. A man *feels* he is a member of a race that is superior to others. A three year old is convinced that his auntie is a Teletubby (true story).

Perception is not reality but can be just as powerful if it seems real to you. As the first grandchild in our family, Brett was doted upon by a host of aunts, uncles, and grandparents. And that love extended beyond our family. If we went to a store or restaurant without Brett, we would be chastised by the locals for not bringing him along. He was loved even by strangers. So years later it was surprising to hear him say that he never *felt* loved. He strayed away from the family and into a life of self-destruction and deception. But thankfully he had a praying mother. It was her persistence in reminding him not only of her love, but the unconditional love of God that restored the hope in his heart and changed his perception of the world around him.

Let the Word of God be your reality check. If your feelings are guiding you to walk contrary to the Word of God, you are headed down a dark path.

To accept "I can't help it" as your defense, is to give your consent to live beneath the privilege and promise of being more than conquerors through Christ Jesus. Change is hard. But with God ALL THINGS ARE POSSIBLE! Make it up in your mind that nothing shall separate you from the love of Christ:

> *"For I am persuaded that neither death, nor life, nor angels, nor principalities, nor powers, nor things present, nor things to come, nor height, nor depth, nor any other creature, shall be able to separate us from the love of God, which is in Christ Jesus our Lord."*
> (Rom.8:38-39)

Be Transformed

To resist change based on the premise that God created you "just as you are" is to be ignorant of the truth that we live in a fallen world. Since the fall of Adam, all men are born into sin. God loves you right where you are, but too much to leave you just as you are. *For what power is there in the resurrection except you die to self and rise up a new creature in Christ Jesus?*

> *"And be not conformed to this world: but be ye transformed by the renewing of your mind, that ye may prove what is that good, and acceptable, and perfect will of God."*
>
> (Rom. 12:2)

We are not to feel our way through life, but to be led by the Spirit. You were created to have dominion over your feelings, thoughts and emotions, not to let them rule over you. It becomes a battle of wills: *God is trying to show you who you are, and you're trying to tell Him how you feel.* In heaven, you will need to check your feelings at the door. As you give an account of your life, feelings will not be there to justify your course, only your actions. It's a fact that the way you feel is very real to you. But in the Kingdom of God, truth trumps fact. Your heart says, "To thine own self be true." But the Apostle Paul said, "Let <u>God</u> be true and every man a liar" (Rom. 3:4). Moreover:

> | We are not to feel our way through life, but to be led by the Spirit. |

> *"The heart is deceitful above all things, and desperately wicked: who can know it? I the Lord search the heart, I try the reins, even to give every man according to the fruit of his doings."*
>
> (Jer. 17:9)

Don't be fooled by your feelings. Want to overcome? Walk in the Spirit!

> *"For if you live after the flesh, ye shall die; but if ye through the Spirit mortify the deeds of the body, ye shall live. For as many as are led by the Spirit of God, they are the sons of God. For ye have not received the spirit of bondage again to fear; but ye have received the Spirit of adoption, whereby we cry, Abba, Father."*
>
> (Rom. 8:13-15)

Will you be overtaken, or will you be an overcomer?

If you are being ruled by your feelings, addictions, or habits, and want to be free, consider this inspiring testimony:

> *A powerful and respected evangelist had a hectic traveling schedule. During one stop, he checked into a hotel and logged on to his computer. While searching the Internet, a shocking thing happened. An X-rated site popped up on his screen. He had never understood how or why people could be hooked on pornography. It was so ... dirty. But in one split second of looking at this pop-up, he was hooked. He said it reached out beyond the screen and, without asking his permission, drew him in, or more like snatched him in. He wanted more. Even though something within him knew that it was wrong, he liked the feeling. Besides, who else would ever know?*

A decision was made. A simple whispering of "God help me" defined his choice. He found the strength to rise out of his chair. He fled the room and walked outside of the hotel. He found himself at a convenience store where the Lord instructed him to purchase some grape juice and crackers. He returned to the hotel room and sat back in front of the computer screen with the pornographic site still displayed. And right there, he took communion. He raised the grape juice up to that very screen and commanded pornography to bow to the name of Jesus, and lust to submit to the powerful blood of Jesus.

One last thing, he called his wife and told her exactly what happened.

That did it. He was free of his feelings.

Turn Around

If you find that you have taken a turn down the wrong path, your mistakes do not have to be fatal:

- Recognize and acknowledge you made a bad choice. Don't keep trying to justify it or make sense of it.

- Take corrective actions and counter measures to get back on course.
- Look back and say to someone else, "Don't come this way."
- Never return to that same path.

> Turning your mistakes into messages that help others can help define your purpose.

Turning your mistakes into messages that help others can help define your purpose. For example, it is evident that our current generation lacks a clearly defined concept of love. In today's contemporary music, love is synonymous with sex. Somebody's got to tell our young people that "Reasons" is not a love song! A true demonstration of love is missing from our music and the big screen. What can you share to enlighten someone and keep them from repeating mistakes you have made? Deliver the word. *Your misery may just become your ministry!*

Change Is Tough, But Rewarding

So why all the hoopla about change? I'm as progressive as the next person, you say. But it has been proven that we all resist change.

> *"If you look at people after coronary-artery bypass grafting two years later, 90% of them have not changed their lifestyle."*
> – Dr. Edward Miller, Dean/CEO Johns Hopkins Medicine

Conventional wisdom says that crisis is a powerful motivator for change, but even severe heart disease doesn't seem to motivate. What is it about us that resists change even when we know it is in our own vital interest?

There Is No Growth Without Change – Broccoli-Cheese Casserole

Oh, the look on a toddler's face when he or she is introduced to those all important green vegetables. But as we mature, we (hopefully) begin to want more of what's best for us, not just the junk that stimulates our taste buds while adding no value to nutrition or growth.

In the elementary school chorus we sang a lively little tune called "Born Free." It gave the sense of living life free from responsibility, order, and authority. That was elementary school. But in the words of comedienne Joan Rivers, "Oh, grow up!" Real life is being free to *grow*.

> There is no growth without change.

Who Moved My Cheese? is a story about unexpected change that takes place in a Maze where four amusing characters look for "Cheese" – a metaphor for what we want in life. Each of us has our own idea of what Cheese is (career, relationship, money, house, etc.), but once we find it, we get attached to it. And if we ever lose it, it can be very traumatic. You must decide if you will be one of the characters that continues the same old routines, even though everything around him is changing, or if you develop the flexibility to succeed in changing times.

No doubt, I am a person of comfort and routine. But I made the choice to embrace change and adopt an attitude of flexibility. To my surprise, I was asked to serve as the department Process Leader, helping our employees stop performing low-value activities and identify more efficient processes. My team's new ways of thinking resulted in a savings for our company of a couple of cool millions. How exciting was that? Not only was I taking change to heart, but was leading others through it!

The cherry on the sundae was when my new boss thanked me during my performance evaluation for being "teachable."

Worth The Risk

Weight gain was a new issue for me. Since childhood, I had never been able to gain weight, even with special vitamins, programs, or power shakes. "That girl couldn't gain weight if she worked in a candy factory," Mom would say. Imagine her surprise when I took my first real summer job in a department store candy factory. It proved Mom right; I never gained a pound.

All that changed following a sudden illness when the doctor's treatment plan included synthetic hormones that instantly caused me to pack on the pounds. The reaction from friends when I first began to speak of dieting was, "Girl please, you don't know what fat is!" But at thirty pounds overweight I was welcomed into all the latest diet craze circles. I tried it all. Low fat, low carb, no carb, and a daily cardio routine – all that while continuously, well, gaining.

One morning I got dressed for work, threw my purse onto the passenger's seat of the car, and backed down the driveway. I was thinking of how futile my efforts had been to lose weight over the past two years. Just as I turned out of the subdivision I heard the Lord say, "Try me." This shocked me. All my efforts up until now I had done "in the name of Jesus." Hadn't I?

Then Sister's face popped up in a bubble over my head. How many times had she pleaded with me to let her balance my hormones naturally? I should be ashamed to say, but the only thing that got me to make the change was when the prescription was no longer covered by my insurance. I called Sister from the pharmacy drive-through and asked just how soon we could start her plan.

> Risk is more than letting go; it is learning to trust there is something greater.

It was like a miracle! I was down five pounds the first week, seven the next, then eleven. Once I hit the gym, I dropped three dress sizes in four months! I was beginning to look and feel like myself. I couldn't believe I had held on to something that wasn't good for me just because I was afraid to take the risk and try something better.

Risk is more than letting go; it is learning to trust there is something greater.

Sometimes the answer is right in front of you. Sometimes the answer *is* you.

Not By Might—My Spirit Is Willing, But ...

You may be reading along and thinking that this all sounds great and certainly sounds like something you probably should do. But, you argue,

I just can't seem to motivate myself. How do I get to the point where I truly *want* change?

The Word of God acknowledges that even when our human spirit is willing, our flesh is weak. It further says that our flesh and the Spirit are at war "...so that you cannot do the things you would" (Gal. 5:17). Paul explained it something like this: I've become aware that in my flesh dwells no good thing. The will to do good is within me, but how to perform the good – I can't find it! But the evil that I don't want to do, that I do." (Go figure.)

What to do?

Pray that the Lord will draw you to His will. I pray daily that He gives me a willing heart and an obedient spirit. It helps to sing songs with the words "Yes, Lord" in the lyrics, like Sandra Crouch's "Completely Yes", or the Clark Sisters "Lord, Give me a Praying Spirit."

I sometimes put Natalie Grant's "Breathe On Me" (power of God, come in and change me), or "Break Me Lord," on repeat and just lie there until it begins to sink in and my heart softens. I need Him to break my will and place His desire within me. Sometimes it feels like a thorn in my heart, but I know that when His will takes root, it will flourish into something beautiful. The song ends so sweetly, *"Draw me, Lord, and I'll run after you."* Like the Song of Solomon, I want Him to draw me like sweet perfume. I know that as He draws me, I will gain strength to run after Him.

> *"...thy name is as ointments poured forth...Draw me, we will run after thee:"*
>
> (Song of Sol. 1:3-4)

Fast Forward

You might consider fasting. Fasting has great benefits. First, it cleanses. Not just physically, but mentally, emotionally, and spiritually. Secondly, it disciplines. Did you know that denying the flesh can put you more in tune with your spiritual nature (the real you) and with the Spirit of God? This act of sacrifice and submission will open your spirit and make the soil of your heart soft and fertile for planting—ready to receive the will of God.

We forget that *we can only overcome through the power of the Holy Spirit and His grace.* As indicated in the Scriptures, we are not to rely on ourselves. Insert your name below:

> *Then he answered and spake unto me, saying, this is the word of the Lord unto (_____), saying, not by might, nor by power, but by my Spirit, saith the Lord of hosts. Who art thou, O great mountain? Before (_____) thou shalt become a plain:"*

(Zech. 4:6-7)

Order My Steps

> *The steps of a good man are ordered by the Lord:"*
>
> Ps. 37:23

Life is a book that reveals its contents one page at a time. This really is a faith walk. God does not provide blueprints. When you take one step toward your destiny, the Lord will illuminate the path for your next step. Step by step, you'll begin to see the plan unfold. Whatever you need to fulfill your purpose for today, you already have. What you need for the next part of your journey will show up when you take the next step.

Adversity will also show up along your path, but just keep moving. The enemy strategizes to:

- Steer or lure you down the wrong path
- Disguise or blind you to your chosen path
- Cut off your path to keep you from moving forward, cause you to turn back, or go in a lesser direction

Stay on course. Do not be tempted by the enemy's tactics. Be confident in the dream God has placed in your heart and hold fast.

"And we know that all things work together for good to them that love God, to them who are the called according to His purpose."

(Rom. 8:28)

> The stairway to greatness is at your feet, there to climb from right where you are.

When you are operating according to God's plan, your steps are ordered by Him. He will open doors that no man can shut and close doors that conflict with His plan for you.

What Is Greatness?

The title of this chapter hints at the answer, that *making necessary changes in our lives sets us on the path to greatness*. It is a growth process of accomplishing, giving back, learning, and teaching. Remember, growth is the purpose of the journey, not a single destination in itself. Character is a mark of greatness, so are charity, integrity, resilience, and overcoming selfishness and fear.

To us, greatness seems lofty, elusive and unreachable. We simply don't know where to begin. Is it over there, where someone else we know achieved success? Maybe it's over there. Maybe it's closer than you think. The stairway to greatness is at your feet, there to climb from right where you are.

We get confused. Instead of striving to be great, we should seek to become vessels fit for the Master's use. Greatness is the ability to influence change, even if in one person. But you can't change the world until you change your own mindset. Don't become consumed with self-promotion, power, or blind ambition. Yielding and adapting to His will, *becoming teachable, useable, and available is your job*. The hand of God will make you great!

Letter To The Present

It's time to write your second letter.

In this letter you will outline the changes you are committed to making and share it with another person. You may find it helpful having someone check your progress and hold you accountable to your goals. Choose someone who will commit to following up with you in a specified amount of time. Using the *"Letter to the Present" template at the end of the chapter,* prepare one copy for yourself and one for the other person. At the appointed time, you will meet and discuss your challenges, progress, and perhaps identify new goals. It will be interesting to note if they see a change in you.

Reflections Of The Journey

- There is no growth without change.
- The pain in your life will persist until you change your actions or thinking.
- We are not to feel our way through life, but be led by the Spirit.
- God loves you right where you are, but too much to leave you just as you are.
- Pray daily that He gives you a willing heart and an obedient spirit.
- Change is hard. But with God ALL THINGS ARE POSSIBLE!
- Turning your mistakes into messages that help others can help define your purpose.
- The stairway to greatness is at your feet, there to climb from right where you are.

The Journey Continues . . .

Letter To The Present

There is no growth without change.

In your own words describe a key area of change you will make and how. Provide a copy to a friend or accountability partner who will check your progress and hold you accountable to your goals. Select a follow up date that is easy to remember such as your birthday or New Year's Day. On that date, have a discussion about your progress.

Your Name: _____

Accountability Partner: _____

Date of Letter: _____/_____/_____
Review Date: _____/_____/_____

_____

_____

_____

_____

_____

_____

_____

_____ _____
Signature   Date

Chapter 9
Who's In Your Life?

People around us can make a difference as to whether we stay on course in achieving our destinies. Be aware that people come into our lives for a reason. Whenever people suddenly appear in your life, you should ask yourself why. Don't take for granted that they should be there or that they mean you good.

> *"Satan uses people to tempt us or cause us to fall. God uses the same to try and make us strong."*
>
> – Ruth Bell Graham

Who's in your life? Why were they sent to you ... to help or to hinder? You have a right, as well as a responsibility, to ask.

The infamous Delilah was sent to Samson, not to help him, but to use her beauty and deceptive powers to cause him to lose his supernatural strength so he would be ineffective for God's pur-

> Who's in your life? Why were they sent to you ... to help or to hinder?

poses. In contrast, Barnabas, a first-century missionary, had a mighty soul-winning ministry. But he went looking for Paul (also called Saul), and together they preached and made many disciples in Antioch, the place where the disciples were first called Christians.

Who is looking for you to help make your vision great?

Gen.14: 18-23 gives an account of two new acquaintances in Abram's life. Both offered to bless him. Abram received blessings from one, but refused the other. From Melchizedek, king of Salem, and the priest of the most high God, he not only received blessings but gave him a tenth of his spoils of war. In the very next verse, Abram refused to take even a thread of a shoe latchet from the king of Sodom, lest he should say, "I have made Abram rich."

Learn to discern. While your enemies may befriend you as a tactic, do not become comfortable with them. Recognize them for who they are.

Nevertheless, adversaries can serve an important purpose. *God uses our enemies to make us strong and to elevate us.* David, without his defeating the lion, the bear and Goliath, would have simply remained a shepherd boy. His victory over his adversaries made him strong. They came to prove him. They came to make him king. That Goliath in your life may be the key to your success!

Who Has Your Ear?

Decisions affecting your life can not be made based on the thoughts and opinions of others. While you may be wise to seek input from a few trustworthy sources, God's plan for your life is not a democracy; the majority does not rule. Remember all the pageantry surrounding Jesus' entrance into Jerusalem as the crowd shouted "Hosanna to the King?" Three days later they were shouting "Crucify him!" Peter loved Jesus and walked with Him faithfully but abandoned Him in His greatest hour of need, the crucifixion.

Thankfully, God does bring people along side us to support and be a resource to us. But as sincere as their efforts may be, you cannot entrust your destiny to another human being. No human mind can know the fullness of all that God has in store for your life. Give Him your ear.

Divine Connections

In God's divine plan people need people, and connect with one another. It's critical to our success. "The whole body is fitted together perfectly. As each part does its own special work, it helps the other parts grow, so that the whole body is healthy and growing and full of love" (Eph. 4:16).

If your vision is truly from God, it will require you to connect with other people. In this way, we sort of connect the dots in our lives. If you can accomplish your vision all by yourself, you should seriously question whether it is of God. You never know who is assigned to bless you, promote you, or be the missing link that will usher you into your destiny. Favor may come from the most unlikely sources. Never assume, underestimate, or overlook the possibilities and potential in people around you. You never know what someone's full potential is.

Your divine connection could be a mentor with wise words, an investor with funds, or someone who can give you access to a person you need to know. Favor with the right person at the right time is more valuable than money. *We are bridges to one another's future.*

So even though you may not know exactly whom God will use to connect you to your vision, why not begin to pray for them now, that their steps will be ordered by the Lord and that they will begin to walk in divine purpose? And I hope that when you find you have the resources someone else needs to bring them one step closer to their destiny, you'll be gracious.

> We are bridges to one another's future.

Now that's divine!

Anointing For Purpose

When the Lord instructed Moses to build a tabernacle of worship in the wilderness, Moses was perplexed because he lacked the skills required to complete the task. But God let Moses in on a little secret; He had already anointed those around Moses with the abilities to perform the necessary tasks. According to Ex. 31:3-11: "And I have filled him with the

Spirit of God, in wisdom, and in understanding, and in knowledge ... to work in all manner of workmanship...and in all the hearts of all that are wise hearted I have put wisdom, that they may make all that I have commanded thee."

Throughout the chapter are examples of how the Lord gave anointings for people to do all manner of works – carpentry, jewelry, masonry, garments and perfume. All to perform the purpose of the Lord according to the vision He had given Moses. When you begin to move in purpose, the Lord will place others around you who possess all that you need to fulfill the vision.

Our good God of excellence thinks of everything!

We Are Instruments

Think of yourself as an instrument, an inanimate object like a flute or a trumpet, that is useless until the breath of life is blown into it. Then it makes beautiful sounds. More accurately, that breath is blown *through* it. If it was contained inside the instrument, no one would hear it. But when it emerges, the world is blessed.

When many instruments release coordinated sounds together we have harmony—we become a symphony.

What a masterpiece we are!

That's What Friends Are For

Relationships can be powerful influences in our lives. Sometimes in relationships, we expect one individual (friend, spouse, parent, etc.) to be all things to us. Not only can they not live up to these expectations, they are not called to do so. God did not design it that way, lest we make gods of one another. In the very center of the Bible we find these words:

> "It is better to trust in the Lord that to put confidence in man."
> (Ps.118:8)

Sometimes our sight is so limited that we can only see as far as the hand that feeds us. Just remember, regardless of whom your blessings flow through, God is your source. Look to Him.

Before we allow our frustrations to ruin our friendships, we should learn to appreciate the unique qualities each brings to the relationship. For example, you may have a wonderful prayer partner who has helped you through spiritual warfare; another who is an inspiration, believes in your dreams and won't let you do less than your best; a problem solver who offers wisdom and practicality; a fun-loving friend who helps you de-stress and relax; or a mentor who will give you advice and direction while "keeping it real."

> Regardless of whom your blessings flow through, God is your source.

In my circle, one of my friends is always inspiring, energized, spiritually upbeat, full of hope and creativity, while another is my Zen friend. She is always cool, level headed, easygoing and great to kick back with. Sister, among other things, is definitely my comic relief. She always seems to send me little pick-me-ups just when I need them. Like this email she sent during a stressful workday:

So what if your prayer partner never wants to do anything fun with you? She's watching for your soul! Understand that your fun-loving companion may not tell you that spandex is no longer your friend, but your mentor will. *Likewise, what role has God intended for you to fulfill in someone else's life? Are you out of place?* Do you find that you are attempting to be all things to all people? Remember, a friend *loves* at all times – not a friend *does* at all times. Maybe we should consider having fewer girlfriends and more God-friends.

We must be careful to glean only what God intends from our relationships. His intentions are for His power to work through others to bless you. He never intends for any one human being to be the sole source of your needs. Never give any individual that much power over your life.

Some Interesting Observations Written By Kids

Q: How do you decide who to marry?

A: You got to find a girl who likes the same stuff. Like, if you like sports, she should like it that you like sports, and keep the chips and dip coming.
-- Alan, age 10

Q: What is the right age to get married?

A: No age is good to get married at. You got to be a fool to get married.
-- Freddie, age 6

Q: How can a stranger tell if two people are married?

A: You might have to guess, based on whether they seem to be yelling at the same kids.
-- Derrick, age 8

Q: What do you think your mom and dad have in common?

A: Both don't want any more kids.
-- Lori, age 8

Q: What do most people do on a date?

A: On the first date, they just tell each other lies and that usually gets them interested enough to go for a second date.
-- Martin, age 10

Q: When is it okay to kiss someone?

A: When they're rich.
-- Pam, age 7

Q: How would the world be different if people didn't get married?

A: There sure would be a lot of kids to explain, wouldn't there?
-- Kelvin, age 8

Everyday Heroes (Take My Sister – Please!)

When I think of all the people who have showered my life with blessings, who have loved enough, cared enough and shared enough, I am touched beyond words. We should recognize ordinary people who have impacted our lives every day in great or small ways.

We are shaped and influenced by people around us early in life. I do believe that without Sister I would have been a different person, extremely introverted and withdrawn. My brother, Ted, played a different but very significant role in my life as well.

Big brothers are notorious for picking on their younger siblings and coercing them to do foolish things. Mine was no different. Like his favorite game where he was the king and Sister and I were peasants in the land. We were required to obey and pay him tribute in fried bologna sandwiches.

And how about the permanent scar I earned from the day he and Sister reluctantly allowed me to play Tarzan and Jane, only I was Cheetah. As they instructed, I climbed to the top bunk bed, beat my chest, let out the Tarzan yell, jumped, and–splat! They had moved the roll-away bed and I made impact with the linoleum floor. Today I bear stitches where my tooth went through my bottom lip.

Ah, the good ol' days!

But there's lots to credit my big brother for, including inspiring my early appreciation of music and for literally pushing me out in front of the music. Ted was a drummer, playing in the school marching band as well as in local R&B bands. Somehow, whatever he was doing, he'd convince people to let me be a part of it. Ted had influence that way. Even with our parents! How else would they let their baby girl sing in nightclubs at age fourteen? That took some doing. "The Splendors" would fix me up to look like Diana Ross. Lots of swirly gowns, tons of eye make-up and big, big hair were what got me past the front-door scrutiny of the nightclub owners.

One night, Mom and Dad came to one of our gigs at the Hollywood Club. The band leader announced that our parents were in the house and dedicated a song to them. Then the bass guitar started in and our gowns swayed to the deep, rhythmic thumping. Looking behind me and seeing Teddy's afro towering over the cymbals gave me confidence. At their front row table, Mom and Dad were swaying too. That is, until I took center stage, cooing one of Smokey Robinson's classics. It started off nice and easy, but the lyrics about a woman and her lover were a bit spicy and enticing.

Dad started to squirm.

I did a little dip at the part about "getting dowwwn" with my lover.

Mom's mouth went into a big "O."

Their expressions puzzled me. I had no idea what those words I meant. I was just singing a melodious tune, or so I thought. I got to the hook and threw my hips side to side.

Yeah (Do it baby)!

Dad jumped up, headed straight for the bar, and never came back. When our break came, I asked Ted where our folks had gone. He made a joke that it was past their bedtime.

Well, my parents let me continue performing, but never came to another show.

With my brother's guidance, I began to audition for other opportunities. Before I knew it, I was in three bands, church and school choirs, and the majorettes.

When I started college, Dad wanted me to quit everything. Mom let it be our little secret that I was still in one band. But a visitor from our hometown poked her head in Dad's hospital room where he was recovering from a stroke and announced, "Ted, your baby girl is tearing up the Crazy Quilt nightclub downtown with that Creole Lady Marmalade song. You must be so proud!" Mom started fanning him, afraid he was going to have another stroke. I quit the band.

Eventually, I would make my own choices and decided that gospel music was my true calling. But my brother's musical influence exposed me to a variety of musical genres and experiences while under his protection. He kept the music alive inside of me until I decided which route I wanted to go.

Somebody's Watching You

"Walking down the hall with someone on the way to get a cup of coffee is an interview."

Working in Human Resources for a national insurance firm was the ultimate employment goal for me, or so I thought. The HR Department Manager interviewed me for his opening, but like everyone said, you just couldn't read him. Paul was the master of the game. He would throw you one question,

> Walking down the hall with someone on the way to get a cup of coffee is an interview.

knowing you would unintentionally give him answers to another. And he was famous for asking questions in such a subtle way that you didn't realize the interview had begun. At the conclusion of the interview, you weren't sure if you had bombed or passed with flying colors.

I finally caught on. Everything I said or did *was* the interview. On day three of our interview in Austin, Paul asked a question that stuck with me more than the others. "Do you think you're ready for this? Because this is a highly visible position, and if I put you in front of the company's leadership before you're ready, it could ruin your entire career." He also told me he was considering one other outstanding candidate. In the end, he chose both of us.

Indeed, it was a challenging position, and because our department was adjacent to the Executive Offices, it was not uncommon to find myself strolling down the hallway with one of the vice presidents. I always kept my conversations brief and polite, as I had been advised.

A few years later, I set my sights on another department. But after being hired for the new position, I was informed that instead I would be working as project assistant for one of the vice presidents. At a regional leadership meeting, Don introduced me in my new assignment, saying he had watched me in my HR role and knew I could do as good a job for him. In fact, he joked that Paul really didn't know how to use me to my full potential. My heart sank right to my pinky-toe hearing the VP say that he had watched me!

I was warned he'd be a tough, difficult boss, but it was the best work experience I had ever had. Later, Don thought I was ready to move on and take on the company's Public Relations function in Houston. I didn't feel qualified, but his little pep talk built up my confidence. On my birthday, I interviewed with the Regional Public Affairs Manager. I got the job!

Again I was told that my new boss would be tough. But as PA Manager, Dean not only trained me, educated me, and bragged on me, but recommended me for many developmental and recognition programs. In his fatherly way, he'd say, "You make the decisions about how to run things in Houston, and I'll support you. Just remember, you have to live with the consequences, good or bad. If you need anything, call me." He was not only giving me the authority, but the permission to make mistakes, to learn and to grow. He was always true to his word.

A few managers came with reputations: "he doesn't respect women"; "she has anger issues"; "he's demeaning." People gave me plenty of warning. But I worked for all of them, and all turned out to be some of the best mentors I've had in my career. The reality is that *some people enter your life and connect you to your rainbow, your promise. Suddenly, you can do what you couldn't do before!* From HR, one path connected with another. My steps were ordered by the Lord. Each step of the way, someone was watching me and waiting to give me favor.

Who is watching you?

Difficult People

Often we find ourselves having to deal with difficult people. A few things I have learned through this experience are:

- Difficult people teach you a lot about yourself. (Oh, you thought you were patient?)
- Sometimes they are sent to force you to go, to move on to other things God has for you.
- Sometimes they are sent to distract you from what God needs you to do right where you are.

You can learn a lot of right things from wrong people. You learn how not to do it when you have a similar opportunity. You can learn from their mistakes even if they don't perceive them as mistakes.

Although you may have been hurt or wronged by a relationship, remember this: *You* decide what to take away from every circumstance in your life, good or bad. That is what empowers you to move from victim to victor.

So, Who Is In Your Life?

Get a mental picture of who's in your life now. Think of the roles they play:

- Who inspires you?
- Who is in your life for a season, maybe just to bless you in passing or exchange blessings?
- Who must you disconnect from?
- Who is in your life for a long-term, covenant relationship?
- Who has mentored you?
- Who is your inner court circle?
- Who is your cheerleader?
- Who keeps you spiritually grounded?

Take inventory in the "Who's In Your Life' end of chapter exercise. Ask the Lord to show you who is out of place. Ask him to show you how to disconnect. He will give you the courage and grace you need to follow through.

On the other hand, who has attempted to play a constructive role in your life, but you failed to recognize it, or may even have rejected it? If this is a person God has chosen to bless you and take you to the next level, if your destiny is locked up in that person, then say like Jacob, "I won't let go until you bless me." Or like Ruth, who refused to disconnect from Naomi, "Entreat me not to leave you…" Something in Ruth wanted to stay bonded to Naomi. Had she let go, her Boaz would never have entered her life (see Ruth 1-4).

The Lord sends people among us to help us on our journey. He has predestined people to intercept our paths at the appointed time to help us meet our destiny. On Abraham's journey, he was blessed, celebrated, and refreshed by an encounter with Melchizedek, the high priest. That is the only mention of the two encountering each other. A blessing in passing.

> He has predestined people to intercept our paths at the appointed time to help us meet our destiny.

Please accept that *some people are sent into our lives for only a season*. They walk one particular path with you along your journey, and then move on. So once you turn the corner, you need to let go of their hand. God is up ahead showing you to a new path.

Reach for Him.

Time To De-Tox

In this health-conscious age of cleansing our internal organs and exfoliating dead skin, let's not forget about our social environments. We are products of these environments. Good or bad, you will start to emulate those around you and eventually duplicate it in others.

It was once told to me that *as you grow in life, your friends will either grow or go*. A test of whether you've grown or changed is: Has your personal phone book changed over the years?

When you find yourself in a period of weakness, don't turn to weak people for help. You can't expect people who think small to encourage you to dream big. Don't spend time with negative, complaining, naysayers. Surround yourself with people who enrich your life—those who reflect your current values, goals, interests and lifestyle.

What's the best advice you received this year? If you can't answer, you've either not been listening or you've been surrounding yourself with wrong people!

Rid yourself of toxic relationships, those that drain you of your time, energy, and resources, cause you to fall into temptation, and those that discourage change and growth in your life. And something to remember about those chronic gossipers: if they're telling you negative things about someone else, they're telling someone else negative things about you! Don't hang around people who constantly remind you of your past—who you were, what you've done. Spend your time with those who are excited about your future and where you're going in life.

A popular saying that's worth repeating is: Why stay where you're simply tolerated? Move on to where you are celebrated!

Pray now about who is in your life.

Another Of Sister's Pick-Me-Ups:

Subject: Tragic Loss

It is with the saddest heart that I pass on the following news:

Please join me in remembering a great icon of the culinary community. The Pillsbury Doughboy died yesterday of a yeast infection and complications from repeated pokes in the belly. He was 71. Dough Boy is survived by his wife, Play Dough and his two children, John Dough and Jane Dough, who has a bun in the oven. He is also survived by his elderly father, Pop Tart. Dough Boy was buried in a lightly greased coffin.

Dozens of celebrities turned out to pay their respects, including Mrs. Butterworth, Hungry Jack, The California Raisins, Betty Crocker, the Hostess Twinkies, and Captain Crunch. The grave site was piled high with flours. Aunt Jemima delivered the eulogy and lovingly described Dough Boy as a man who never knew how much he was kneaded. Dough Boy rose quickly in show business, but his later life was filled with turnovers. He was not considered a very smart cookie, wasting much of his dough on half-baked schemes.

Despite being a little flaky at times, he still, as a crusty old man, was considered a roll model for millions.

The funeral was held at 3:50 for about 20 minutes.

Reflections Of The Journey

- When people suddenly appear in your life, you should ask yourself why.

- Good or bad, you will begin to emulate those around you and eventually duplicate it in others.

- Adversaries serve a purpose. God uses our enemies to make us strong and to elevate us.

- You cannot fully entrust your destiny to another human being.

- We are bridges to one another's future. Your vision will require you to connect with other people.

- Some people are sent into our lives for only a season.

- Learn to appreciate the unique qualities each relationship brings to your life.

- God has predestined people to intercept your path at the appointed time to help you meet your destiny.

- Regardless of who your blessings flow through, God is your source. Look to Him.

The Journey Continues . . .

Exercise

Who's In Your Life?

*Get a mental picture of who's in your life now.
Think of the roles they play. Take inventory:*

Who inspires you to dream? _____

Who is your prayer partner? _____

Who speaks truth to you? _____

Who relaxes and refreshes you? _____

Who keeps you spiritually grounded? _____

Who must you disconnect from? _____

Who has mentored you? _____

Who is your inner-court circle? _____

Who is your mentee? _____

Who is your cheerleader? _____

Who is in your life for a season, maybe just in passing to bless you or exchange blessings? _____

Who is in your life for a long-term covenant relationship? _____

Ask the Lord to show you who is out of place.

Chapter 10
Life is a Trip

Life is an adventure! We are all travelers with many paths to choose from. How do we find the path that is right for us? In our thinking, it may seem just as good to go it alone. After all, we are intelligent beings. Why do we need God? Well, He has wisdom and insight that you don't have. He knows the path that is set before you, including every stumbling block, every barrier, every enemy and pitfall. He has the eagle-eye advantage. He sits high and looks low. He cautions us not to lean to our own understanding, but to trust Him to direct our path.

> *"Trust in the Lord with all thine heart and lean not unto thine own understanding. In all thy ways acknowledge Him, and He shall direct thy paths."*
>
> Prov. 3:5, 6

Take a look at your present day circumstances. I'm sure you'll conclude that you could benefit from such supernatural guidance – couldn't you?

Rules of the Road

Be prepared for the journey. You can't always count on the other guy for roadside assistance. Don't be guilty of D.U.I. Driving Under the Influence (of others), without making preparations of your own.

Driving the 101 around Phoenix was a new experience for me. It's strange to see beautiful mountains peering between tall buildings along the freeway. But I was interrupted by the girls shouting from the back seat, "Christian doesn't have his seat belt on!" I used to tell them when they were little that Aunt Stacie's car wouldn't go if all seat belts weren't fastened. So I let the car slow to a sputter until Christian, my four year old godson, understood. After quickly buckling in, he wanted me to see firsthand:

> "Sashee, look at me. I put my seat belt on!"
>
> "Yes, I can tell, Christian because the car is driving really well now. Thank you!"
>
> "But I want you to turn around and look."
>
> "Honey, Aunt Stacie can't turn around right now because she has to watch the road, okay?"
>
> (Pause)
>
> "No, no. I'll watch the road for you, Sashee!"

Scary, huh? We all laughed at the thought of me explaining to the officer that I was looking behind me while a toddler was directing me on the road. Yet, sometimes in real life we are guilty of allowing someone else, who has no clue where we are headed, to advise us on how to get through life. As a responsible driver, the first rule of the road is you must prepare and plan for your trip.

Signs

Life's highway is filled with signs that give us instructions, if only we will take heed.

Many times after I've made a mistake, I've looked back and realized there were signs. Whether they were subtle warnings or big, flashing neon lights, I had somehow excused them away. Probably because I desired something in my flesh and hoped the Lord would go along with it. Other times, I simply wasn't paying attention. In today's world, it's easy to get distracted by all that's going on around us, even by our own feelings and emotions.

One night I was lying in bed, thinking about my mistakes, miseries, and failures. A single tear trickled down my cheek (it was great drama). Suddenly, I sat straight up in bed. I heard the Lord say very clearly, "I need your full attention!" It was as startling, as if you were driving along and about to miss a turn or run a red light, and your driving instructor yells, "Stop!" In other words, the Lord was saying, "I've got plans for you, but if you're not alert to my instructions, you could miss out on the wonderful blessings along the road of life".

Provision for the Vision

Provision is available to those who step out and move in purpose. Did you know that your provision is waiting for you along your path of purpose? But to reach it, you must move toward it and intersect it.

While living in Pittsburgh during one of the lowest times in my life, I had just started a new job with a great company. But the lack of training and workload left me frazzled. The senior customer service reps came to me in secret and offered their advice and assistance. They'd remark: "We thought you would have quit by now." A few months later, a new training program was implemented. The new trainees received special training, went on field trips, and discussed customer scenarios together. I was not included, though I asked to be. These new recruits enjoyed scheduled salary increases and were protected from overwork by having a limit to the number of new customer claim files they could receive. But not me.

> Did you know that your provision is waiting for you along your path of purpose?

I was praying desperately for change when a visiting evangelist spoke a powerful word over me: "Elevation & Increase"! I quickly grabbed on to that word, not knowing how God would bring it to pass. Not long after, I was having a casual conversation with a seasoned co-worker who made me aware that Personnel still had me in trainee status. During that time period, four or five bosses had barely noticed I was there. No wonder! But when I brought this to my current manager's attention, the paperwork for my promotion was processed effective immediately. *I had stepped onto the path of provision by receiving the word of the Lord.*

A few weeks later, I was unexpectedly sent to Texas on catastrophe duty to assist with claims resulting from severe flooding. Within twenty-four hours, I was in Houston calling Sister to let her know I was in her city. My supervisor, Rosemary, really liked me and kept requesting extensions so that I worked catastrophe duty all summer long. I had no idea that "storm troopers" were paid money in addition to their regular salary to make this sacrifice. *I just followed the path.*

TWA (Traveling with the Angels)

I sure enjoyed the time I was able to spend with Sister and the kids. My little niece showed me a drawing she had made, with Aunt Stacie flying to Houston to live permanently. Angels were flying beside the plane.

On my last day of storm duty, Rosemary announced to the office, "All y'all can come to lunch if you want to, but I ain't payin' for nobody but Stacie." (This is proper Texas English.) The whole office came, and made me promise that I would put in for a transfer back to Houston. I promised, knowing that there were no current openings. *Said who?* As soon as we returned to the office and I began packing my desk, I heard Rosemary scream! She came dashing out of her office telling everyone that she had just *unexpectedly been given the approval to increase her staff – by one.*

"Gee, Lord. That was quick!" I thought. But *He was just waiting for me to verbally agree with what He had already planned for me,* and then it all started to fall into place. Upon my return to Pittsburgh from storm duty, I discovered that my supervisor had been replaced by a former co-worker and friend. I kept laughing and saying, "Seriously, James? You're my new boss?" But his promotion was key to the plan's success. You see, the former supervisor never approved transfers. But James, against the advice of upper management, granted the approval. I was headed back to Texas quicker than you could say BBQ. There I was, flying the friendly skies with the angels leading the way, just like my little niece's picture. (After that, we all tried to exploit her little gift by having her draw pictures of things we wanted like houses and cars, but she would only draw what was in her heart.) I'm glad I was.

The catastrophe duty check I received was more than enough to cover the moving costs. There was *provision for the vision*. There was *elevation and increase* just as God's messenger had spoken a few months before.

Provision lines the path the Lord has set before us. I didn't know what God had in mind, but *God knew and He made the way*. All the right people were in place. Those that were obstacles were moved and replaced with someone more in sync with God's plan. As for Rosemary, as soon as I arrived she called me in to apologize, because she had just accepted a promotion and would not be my supervisor. I believe the Lord had the promotion for her all along, but kept her there long enough to facilitate my transfer to Texas.

My new supervisor recognized strengths I didn't even know I had. Before long, I was helping to train others. I gained confidence and within a couple of years, when I was ready to move into Human Resources, she mentored me, believed in me, and coached me into a place I was destined to be. In my former location I was overlooked, over burdened, and unappreciated. But here, I was celebrated, mentored and promoted. *I had favor!*

A New Path

Spaghetti City. That's what people often call Houston. It is a humongous network of freeways. The weather on the Gulf is incredibly humid and the summer heat is hardly bearable for humans. Vehicles suffer as well. (There are lots of "Car-B-Qs" along the freeways.) But when it rains, it pours, and the land floods very quickly. It's almost nothing to see a car float by on I-10.

When I first arrived in Houston, I saw things I'd never seen in other parts of the country, such as roaches as big as poodles! But if you swat at them, be sure not to miss. You see, no one told me these critters could fly. It's just wrong to start out chasing a roach and end up with it chasing you!

But, I soon learned that *everything's* bigger in Texas. That included state pride. The things usually reserved for tourists in airport gift shops, like ten-gallon hats, Texas t-shirts and rhinestone jewelry; people wear them everyday, everywhere. Women in formal wear and big hair stroll into ballrooms on the arms of their husbands proudly donning jeans with starched creases, big belt buckles, steel-tipped cowboy boots, and, of course, their tallest Texan cowboy hat. Friends who migrated to Texas from the north absolutely despised the arrogance. They said Texans had an attitude, as if they were held to a different standard than the Constitution of the United States.

I had to admit, the culture was so different; Texas felt like another country. Perhaps not, but it certainly was a new and different path.

Move!

Remember how God led the children of Israel through the wilderness as a pillar of cloud by day and a pillar of fire by night? As long as they moved where the Lord led them, they knew their needs would be met and they would be fed manna from heaven daily. If they stayed behind, they would be on their own with no promise of provision. God promises provision when we move in purpose. *You can't live forever off the residue of where God has been, what He once touched, or where He once moved.* In other words, you can't afford to lag behind and get comfortable.

> You can't live forever off the residue of where God has been, what He once touched, or where He once moved.

There's no provision there, no protection, and no promise.

Move with the glory cloud!

It's important to note in my example that the move was geographical. But much, much, more often, God moves us spiritually or mentally, away from old ways of thinking. If you're considering relocation to advance your career, ministry, or other venture, think about this: is the opportunity to GO an opportunity to GROW?

You may feel that God has forsaken you, but you simply have not moved on to your place of provision. If you're living an unfulfilled life, or even a rebellious life, God is not punishing you. He is waiting for you. Move on to the place of obedience where God's rewards and blessings are flowing. Are you are crying out "Woe is me" and "What shall I do"? I have the answer.

Move!

Don't hesitate. Take a look out the window. I think I hear the sound of a big moving van pulling up in your driveway!

Get Directions

> *"Whether you turn to the right or to the left, your ears will hear a voice behind you saying 'This is the way, walk in it."*
>
> (Isa. 30:21, NIV)

We make decisions daily. Most decisions simply require that we "follow peace" (Heb. 12:14), meaning that although the right decision may move you out of your comfort zone, it should not cause you extreme anxiety, confusion, or turmoil. But some decisions are more complex than others. If they are life changing, the wrong decision can cost you.

No worries. Divine direction is available!

Need a word? Here's what to do:

1. **Pray For Guidance.** The assignment of the Holy Spirit is to lead and guide you into all truth. What a privilege! If only we would take advantage of the benefit. He is speaking, if you are seeking (and listening). If it is something you have prayed about before,

go back to the last thing you heard God say. *God will not give a new instruction until you obey the last one.*

2. **Search the Scriptures.** Through the word, God has given us everything that pertains to life and godliness (2 Pet.1:3). Seek diligently and ye shall find. Confirmation of that same word may come to you in your prayer time or across the pulpit on Sunday morning.

> God will not give a new instruction until you obey the last one.

3. **Seek Wisdom.** Do your homework. Research your options. Test the validity and the integrity of the presenter of any opportunities. Pray for godly wisdom and discernment. Be alert. He may confirm His word through the wisdom and insight of others who intersect your path.

4. **Forgive.** *Forgiving others will unstop deaf ears.* Likewise, seek to be forgiven.

5. **Wait with Patience.** Don't jump at the first thing that tickles your ear. Be aware that you initially may just hear the answer "in part," Stay tuned to get the full picture. And something I learned the hard way: deception will reveal itself in time!

6. **Listen.** You have thought it through, now stop thinking, *be still, and listen.*

Life Is Just Like Driving
(Highway Dangers, Roadblocks and Hindrances)

If you think about it, life is a lot like driving:
- First you decide where you want to go.
- Then you figure out how to get there.
- If you go the wrong way, what do you do? Turn around!
- If you get lost, stop and ask for directions
- If the road you're used to traveling is now closed, take a detour.
- Be alert for obstacles along the way!

On Memory Lane

What year are you living in? What events (good or bad) do you frequently reflect on, talk about most, and allow to dominate your thoughts? No one has ever found the path that leads back to the good old days. People who want to revisit their past are either looking for comfort in what they are familiar with, or a place to find answers. You can look back, but you cannot go back. *Forget the former things. You can't move forward driving in reverse.*

> Forget the former things. You can't move forward driving in reverse.

> *"Remember ye not the former things... behold, I will do a new thing."*
>
> (Isa. 43:18, 19)

Blind Spots

We all have areas that need improvement. If left unchecked, these weaknesses can make us vulnerable. They are our blind spots. Be aware of your weaknesses, but focus on your strengths.

> *"And I will bring the blind by a way that they knew not; I will lead them in paths that they have not known: I will make the darkness light before them..."*
>
> (Is 42:16)

Dangerous curves

We are not always warned when life is about to throw us a curve ball. You may hit an unexpected icy patch on the road that sends you spinning. It may be an illness, a job loss, or a legal matter. Buckle up! Stay secure in the Word of God. *He will make the crooked places in your life straight.*

> *"I will go before thee, and make the crooked places straight..."*
>
> (Isa. 45:2)

Crossroads

Choose your path carefully. These are long-term, life-changing, sometimes irreversible decisions; like marriage, career, and health issues. *You are either at a crossroad, just leaving one, or headed toward one.* Look both ways!

Detours

There you are, going full speed ahead down the road toward a special moment you have been working toward and—what? The road is blocked. The sign says Detour. (Oh yes, it happens.) Why? To stop you from succeeding is your first reaction. But consider that it could also be there *to protect you*, to keep you from going down a wrong, dangerous path, or proceeding too soon.

> *"And we know that all things work together for good to them that love God, to them who are the called according to his purpose."*
>
> (Rom. 8:28)

Divine Delay

No one enjoys being stuck in traffic, but some delays are divine. Timing is important. Preparation must meet opportunity.

> *"He hath made everything beautiful in His time…"*
>
> (Eccl. 3:11)

Perhaps the delay is to allow you time to perfect attitudes, skills, or heart matters (to mature you so that you'll be able to handle and hold on to your blessing).

Or maybe you are not in the right place to birth your blessing.

Aside from your own preparation, the right people need to be positioned and prepared to help you succeed. Start praying now for those the Lord has assigned to assist you on your journey, that they will be fully equipped to achieve excellence at the appointed time.

Delay is not necessarily denial.

"Wait" Is An Active Word

Something is happening while you are waiting. God is strengthening your heart!

> *"Wait on the Lord: be of good courage, and He shall strengthen thine heart:"*
>
> (Ps. 27:14)

You are increasing in courage so that you won't fear or be intimidated when you are presented with a challenge or opportunity. While you are waiting, He is strengthening you. Wait is an active word. Make use of the down time by brushing up on skills or helping others. *Wait does not mean becoming desperate and manipulating your circumstances.* Relax, turn on the cruise control and allow the Lord to perfect those things that concern you.

Acceleration

It's a bumpy road, but you've got the spirit to push on through. As you begin to make progress, build on your momentum and intensify your quest in pursuit of your destiny!

Consider these things that can stall your success:

- Accepting substitutions along the way
- Unwillingness to change course
- Distractions
- Self-inflicted wounds - Negative thoughts and words that cause you to be ensnared by the words of your own mouth.

Instead, do these things that give momentum to your success:

- Confess the Word over your situation
- Maintain a winning attitude
- Be in the presence of other achievers
- Adapt quickly to change and unexpected challenges
- Stay focused on your assignment

Rest Stop

Drowsy driving is as dangerous as DUI. Lack of rest can have negative consequences, like the effect on decision making. On occasion, I have made a decision at the end of a long day just to get it off my to-do list. But the next morning when I look at that same situation, I know I would have made very different choices. We should *rest and refresh before making key decisions*.

Safari!

Ever had an experience that was exciting and scary at the same time? You know it is something you want, but you're afraid to go for it. What a crazy feeling. You're on a Safari!

> A Safari is an adventurous journey in pursuit of a goal in unfamiliar territory, often in difficult terrains.

A Safari is an adventurous journey in pursuit of a goal in unfamiliar territory, often in difficult terrains. It is an experience that will open up the world around you. So why don't we don't just go for it? One reason is our belief that we don't deserve it. Fear also plays a part.

Reasons we don't pursue our dream:

- Fear of not getting it
- Fear of getting it
- Fear of losing it
- Fear of inadequacy

Just when you decide to venture out, you start to hear the theme from *Jaws*. Uh-oh, something's coming. You don't know what. You can't see it. Can't hear it. It's a feeling. It's scary. And it's bad! Then up comes the shark! AHHHHH!

I used to run from anything that scared me (how could something that frightens me possibly be good for me?). But the motto of the truly adventurous is, "If it scares you, do it!" That may sound like poor Christian etiquette, but *sometimes the only thing that conquers fear is stepping toward it and "doing" the very thing that scares you.*

Faith In Reverse

We hope in our future. If faith is the vehicle that moves us forward, fear is faith in reverse. Fear says hope is lost. You know you are driving in reverse when the more you step on the gas, the farther you move away from your goal! Fear can be a major hindrance on your journey.

Fear and faith cannot co-exist. You will have to choose to live one reality or the other. *If you are finding it hard to walk in faith, look at the fear in your life.* Determine what the point of entry was, things like:

- Speaking negatively or allowing others to speak it over you
- Astrology
- Psychic readings
- Music, movies, or books that exalt darkness
- A little too much Halloween!

Renounce these things and don't allow them to influence your life again.

Your Safari will bring you challenges, but will also open you to worlds you have never seen. Your vision may be to start a new business, or pursue higher education, or expand your ministry. Accept the challenge to excel and move in faith.

Go ahead, have the adventure of a lifetime!

Go the Distance

Whatever the highway dangers, stay the course. Ask for divine direction and pay attention to the signs. In spite of the hindrances you have encountered along the way, get back on the road! Remember that *defeat is temporary.* Think like a winner and *keep moving in faith!* If you maintain your course, it will be no accident that you will come face to face with your destiny!

Reflections Of The Journey

- On the road of life, don't be guilty of D.U.I. Driving Under the Influence (of others).

- Forget the former things. You can't move forward driving in reverse.

- You can't live forever off the residue of where God has been, what He once touched, or where He once moved.

- Provision is along the path, waiting for you to move toward it and intersect it.

- You are either at a crossroad, just leaving one, or headed toward one.

- "Wait" does not mean becoming desperate and manipulating your circumstances.

- Fear and faith cannot co-exist. You will have to choose to live in one reality or the other.

The Journey Continues . . .

Part III
Sacred Places

"When something ends –
Something new begins!"

Chapter 11
Secrets of the Seasons

Seasons of Your Life - They Change

In Pennsylvania the seasons are clearly defined. When the leaves turn spectacular shades of gold, orange, and ruby that take your breath away, it's fall. When the temperatures drop below freezing and snow blankets the earth, it is undoubtedly winter. But in Texas, the seasonal changes could slip right by you without notice. Sometimes the seasons in our lives are subtle that way. But make no mistake: "To everything there is a season, and a time to every purpose under the heaven" (Eccl. 3:1).

We need to be alert, to be sensitive to the times. Don't get so comfortable where you are that you don't recognize when the seasons in your life are changing. There is a time for everything.

> Don't get so comfortable where you are that you don't recognize when the seasons in your life are changing.

> There is a reason behind every season in your life.

Hallmark gives us a little help in identifying key stages of our lives like sweet sixteen, over the hill at thirty, and silver anniversaries after twenty-five years of marriage. But many times *there will not be a trumpet sound to announce that you are moving from one season to another,* from one level in the spirit to another. There are signs, however. Just like growing out of old clothes, you begin to feel uncomfortable. Your taste changes. Things you used to like to do, places you liked to go, even the kind of people you liked being around are changing. You can't explain it, but something's different. By the end of the summer we are too hot, and longing for fall. By winter's end we are too cold and wishing for spring. There is an awareness, a shifting that tells us we are moving toward new territories, experiences, and dimensions. Grandma used to sing:

> *Time is filled with swift transition*
> *Not of earth unmoved can stand*
> *Build your hopes on things eternal*
> *Hold to God's unchanging hand*

Our instinct is to hold on to what's familiar because we can't imagine there might be something better. But just hold God's hand and let the rest go. *There is a reason behind every season in your life,* which is to perfect those things that concern you that you may obtain the promise or reward for that season, and to qualify you for the next level or season in your life.

The Four Seasons of Life

Let us explore the various seasons, keeping in mind that these *seasons of life are not based on chronological age or calendar years.* You could possibly remain in one season for many years, or experience multiple seasons in a short period of time.

Winter – *Season of "Regrouping"*

> *A time to rest, to die to old ways, thoughts and values. "…their strength is to sit still."*
>
> (Isa. 30:7)

You feel that with the onset of winter an interruption has occurred, slowing you down. You may feel stuck, bitter. Your once vibrant surroundings now seem barren and cold as you are dealing with the difficulties of life. But this can also be a serene time of quiet reflection by the warmth of a fireplace. You will have many questions, but as you move from winter to spring, new revelation will come.

Take advantage of this season of rest to get ready for new growth.

"Winter" is a good time to retrace your steps and rethink your plans. Rearrange and set things in order. Seek wisdom for focus, direction, and spiritual maturity.

Spring – *Season of "Possibilities"*

> *A time of hope and renewal.*

A season of opportunities and open doors has arrived! The blanket of snow has lifted and unveils new potential for a fresh new start. The earth is green and the ground is fertile to begin planting seeds. Spring is also a season of resurrection. Perhaps there are gifts and talents you once buried that the Lord wants to breathe new life into. Start sowing seeds of possibilities. Planting is hard work! Fragrant herbs and blossoms fill the air and keep you invigorated.

"Spring" is a good time to start new projects, plant seeds for new business ventures, make a new friend.

SUMMER – *Season of "Manifestation"*

> *A time to witness the first results of what you planned in winter and sowed in the spring.*

A time of passion and energy for life. A time to dance and embrace. People take notice and interest in your ideas. The summer sun can be draining, but do not faint. You are very close to your harvest time.

> *"And let us not be weary in well doing: for in due season we shall reap, if we faint not."*
>
> (Gal. 6:9)

The summer sun must be balanced with summer rain. Too much sun causes the earth to be parched and dry. Water it with the Word. Nothing like a cool, drenching, summer rain.

"Summer" is a good time to monitor your projects, find ways to keep the momentum going and keep them on course.

Fall – Season of "Harvest"

> *A time to pluck up, to reap.*

A time to enjoy the fruits of your labor. Whether it's a good or bad crop depends on how you lived, what you learned, and how you gave in the former seasons.

Fall is also a time of shaking, shedding, transition, and change. "Fall" is a good time to shed things you've become attached to that may be unhealthy for your journey (habits, attitudes, bad influences, etc.)

What season are *you* in? *(Complete the exercise at the end of the chapter)*

Seasonal Protocol

> *"As long as the earth remains, there will be planting and harvest, cold and heat, summer and winter, day and night."*
>
> (Gen.8:22, NLT)

Life is constantly moving and changing. A few key things to remember:

1. **Know the season you are in and govern yourself accordingly**
   God's promise that the seasons will always continue in the earth also pertains to the cycles we will experience in our lives as long

as we live on the earth. Govern yourself according to the season you are in. Don't take off running when the word to you in this season is stand still, wait and trust. Don't sit too long mourning your past while God is ushering you toward the door to your future.

2. **Recognize when your season is changing, and prepare.**
   Don't be caught looking back or trying to hold on to a past season and miss what God has for you in this season. During winter, rest up for those busy seasons ahead. Want a great fall harvest? Sow your very best seeds in your spring seasons by giving the best of your time, talent, and monetary gifts. Letting go of your former season means you are ready for promotion. When something ends, something new begins!

3. **Recognize that the season you are in may be very different from that of the people around you.**
   Some financial experts recommend a "spending fast" to help people get out of debt and set themselves on a path to prosperity. Just as you would turn down food during a traditional fast, you would not make unnecessary purchases for this season of time. This not only requires discipline but an awareness that you are on a different path than others around you. You can't become jealous when your neighbors are buying new cars and going on elaborate vacations. You will not succeed in your efforts if you go out and try to make those same choices when it's not your season to do so.

4. **Don't judge your life by only one season.**
   Don't allow the pain of one season to destroy the joy of all the rest. If you give up when it's winter, you will miss the promise of your spring, the beauty of your summer, and fulfillment of your fall. Persevere through the difficult times being confident that better times are sure to come "in due season."

"...weeping may endure for a night, but joy cometh in the morning."

(Ps. 30:5)

Reflections Of The Journey

- Don't get so comfortable where you are that you don't recognize when the seasons in your life are changing.

- There will not always be a trumpet sound to announce that you are moving from one season to another.

- There is a reason behind every season in your life, which is to perfect those things that concern you, and to qualify you for the next level or season.

- Know the season you are in and govern yourself accordingly.

- Recognize that the season you are in may be very different from that of the people around you.

- Don't judge your life by the pain of one season.

- When something ends ... Something new begins!

The Journey Continues . . .

Exercise

What Season Are You In?

Check the box beside the season you are in:

❑ **SPRING** - *Season Of "Possibilities"* - *A time of hope and renewal.*
A Good Time To: Start new projects, plant seeds for new business ventures.

❑ **SUMMER** - *Season Of "Manifestation"* - *A time to witness the first results of what you planned in winter and sowed in the spring. People take interest in your ideas.*

A Good Time To: Monitor projects. Find ways to keep the momentum going and keep them on course.

❑ **FALL** - *Season Of "Harvest"* - *A time to pluck up, to reap.*

A Good Time To: Enjoy the fruits of your labor. Shed things you've become attached to that may be unhealthy for your journey (habits, attitudes, bad influences, etc.).

❑ **WINTER** – *Season Of "Regrouping"* - *A time to rest, to die to old ways, thoughts and values.*

A Good Time To: Retrace your steps and rethink your plan. Rearrange and set things in order. Seek wisdom for focus, direction and spiritual maturity.

How will you make the most of your current season?

_____

_____

_____

_____

_____

_____

_____

> "Ah, but a man's reach should exceed his grasp - or what's a heaven for?"
>
> – Robert Browning

Chapter 12
Write the Vision

Get a pen and paper.

This is the critical first step in the process of achieving your dream. If you miss it here, if you don't align yourself with the vision God has for you, you will be off course.

Without vision, we perish (see Ps. 29:18). *Our plans and dreams wither and die inside unless we can clearly visualize what it is we are trying to accomplish.*

> *"If your mind doesn't have a picture of the future, it will replay the past."*
>
> – Dr. Mike Murdock

God's vision for you will be beyond what you are humanly capable of accomplishing. If the vision before you seems like something you can manage fully by yourself, it probably isn't from God, or you are not seeing the fullness of the vision. This assures that you will rely on Him to provide what you need for the vision (the provision), and that there is room for other people whose visions will connect with yours.

The vision from God will always be bigger than you are because God is bigger than you are. At times it will seem like too much; it will be outside of your comfort zone with some elements beyond your abilities. There will come a time when you will say, "I wish God had never shown this to me." There will come a time when you will say, "*Did* God really show this to me?" You will know the vision is from God if it:

- Keeps coming back to you
- Keeps you coming back to God for:
  - Direction
  - Favor
  - Next Steps
  - Open Doors
  - Wisdom
  - Divine Connections

What do you dream of?

What uncommon goals do you wish to achieve? Instead of dwelling on how you wish things were, don't' wish, make a list! Put it in writing. Bring it out of the unseen into the natural realm.

> *"And the LORD answered me, and said, Write the vision, and make it plain upon tablets, that he may run that readeth it. For the vision is yet for an appointed time, but at the end it shall speak, and not lie: though it tarry, wait for it; because it will surely come, it will not tarry.'"*
>
> (Hab. 2:2-3)

> **If you can get it all done tomorrow, it isn't vision.**

It will surely come, but you've got to write it before you run with it. Devote some thought to it. Ask the Lord to reveal it to you. Don't rush it. Remember that vision is long term. If you can get it all done tomorrow, it isn't vision.

Is It Written?

Take a survey of your own. Ask ten people if they have put their life goals in writing. Probably 95 percent do not. Most people dream about it, talk about it, but never record it and commit it to paper. If you do just this much you are ahead of the game! Not just ahead of others, but further along than you were last year or even yesterday.

Find Your Inspiration

You may not be able to just grab that pen and start writing all willy-nilly, expecting something of quality to magically appear. You need to be inspired. Recognize what or who sparks creativity in you. You might want to consider these:

- **Music**. Choose music that will create a backdrop for your thought process rather than to dominate it. Perhaps something instrumental.
- **Reading**. Read something that is motivational or poetic. The book of Psalms may be a good starting place. Also, autobiographies of people who have achieved success may inspire you.
- **Conversation**. Certain people seem to inspire us when we are around them. Have dinner with a friend or someone with whom you find yourself being more positive or more creative in their presence. Someone who makes you feel like you want to dream again and accomplish things you had left undone.
- **Quiet Place.** It is essential that you find a place of quiet reflection. Maybe the back porch swing, or near the pool. Light a candle or have a soothing cup of tea by the fireplace. Find a time and place where you can get alone with God and meditate on what He is speaking to you.

Start simple. Use bullet points, a sketch, a photo, an outline, a conversation you had, or last night's dream. Once you start, the rest will come. Not all at once (you couldn't handle that), but day by day you will begin to see the big picture.

If You Write It, It Will Come

I dreamed of owning a home. I envisioned it would have a certain floor plan, certain style of kitchen, etc., and all at a certain price. I kept a list in my computer of what I desired. My circumstances at the time didn't support my dream. The company I worked for couldn't decide whether to keep me in Austin or relocate me back to Houston. I commuted back and forth several times a month. With the help of a good friend, I found the perfect house for me in Houston, only it was beyond my price range.

Several weeks later, my friend and I visited that same salesman. To our surprise, without any negotiations, he offered the price I was believing for. However, when I got back to Austin, I was told that the company had changed their mind and decided to keep me in Austin. Then the salesman called and said he had misquoted the price by several thousand and the builder would not honor it. But I had a contract which he was bound to honor. On my next trip to Houston, I walked around the entire house and quoted, "Every place the sole of my foot shall tread, the Lord has given me..." (Josh.1:3). On Valentine's Day, I was handed the keys to my new home, at a comparable price and with the floor plan on my wish list. My company had relocated me to Houston with full benefits.

I'm glad I wrote the vision!

What to Expect

As soon as you commit your vision to paper you can expect two things:

> Strategy and adversity will be your companions. Know them well.

1. **Strategy.** The Lord will begin to speak to you about how to achieve the dream. Make it a practice to keep a memo pad or voice recorder of some sort near you at all times. You will need it!

2. **Adversity.** Expect to stir your enemy. Stumbling blocks of every kind will arise. Do not be moved. Adversity simply means you are on to something big.

Strategy and *adversity* will be your companions. Know them well.

How to Tell If Your Vision Is From God

Vision deficiencies in our eyes left undetected or uncorrected can lead to vision loss or blindness. Optometrists recommend an annual vision exam to test the accuracy of our vision. Likewise, we should have regular check-ups for the dreams and vision in our heart.

Be sure to take the vision test at the end of the chapter. If your vision is from God, it should pass the test.

Does your vision:

- Help people
- Utilize your gifts and talents
- Seem bigger than you
- Promote the Kingdom of God, not exalt darkness
- Require you to connect with others
- Keep coming back to you

That last point was mentioned earlier in the chapter. Let's linger there for a moment, shall we? *If the dream in your heart is from God, it will stay in your heart until it comes to fruition.* It could be years. Joseph's dream stayed with him from the time he was in the pit until he reached the palace. When the Lord impressed upon me to write this book, I was very surprised and very, very happy. But not for the reasons you may think. At least not initially. I thought God had finally seen my point—that the music thing just wasn't happening. But this writing thing, I was much more comfortable with that concept. Fine with me, I would much rather stay behind the scenes than to take center stage. Since the CD had been completed, I could move on to my true calling. After finishing a few chapters, the book started to come together. I told myself, "I'm going to write books now, not music. I'm an author, not a singer/ songwriter." I was content.

About that time, our company's had its biggest nationwide event of the year and I was supervising activities for the whole state of Texas. That Friday was crazy. I was frantically placing radio and

> If the dream in your heart is from God, it will stay in your heart until it comes to fruition.

newspaper ads. This was the last possible day to get something on air before show time, so I was waiting for the sales reps to call back and confirm their inventory. I took one last call before lunch.

It was Vivian, an old church friend. She was now a VP for the Houston Rockets organization. She asked if I could sing that night at the Toyota Center, downtown Houston. "Oh, and bring your CDs, they're going to announce it."

Run, but you can't hide. If the vision is from God, it will not leave you.

Are You Pregnant?

Now that you're through gasping, let's continue.

Like most children, my nephew asked his mother how he came into the world. She took her time sharing a beautiful story of love and conception and how she carried him in her *tummy* for nine months. When she finished, all was quiet. Then came his unexpected and emotional outburst. "Why did you swallow me?" He was terrified, as if he thought she might swallow him again. *Perish the thought!*

Children may find it confusing, but mothers are very clear on the matter. You can probably still hear your mother reminding you how her feet swelled, her back ached, and how many hours she labored to deliver you. She remembers like it was yesterday. Ask a mother of any age and she will be able to tell you how she knew she was pregnant, when she started "showing" and how she struggled with sleep that last, uncomfortable month.

The events of the pregnancy are very certain, the stages very memorable. So it is with vision.

You conceive. You know something is alive inside of you. As you nurture the vision, it grows and it shows. *You are not just pursuing a goal, you are birthing a promise!*

> You are not just pursuing a goal, you are birthing a promise!

While pregnant with your vision, you may wake up in the early stages with morning sickness—meaning, you may have regrets. "What was

I thinking? I can't do this right now. I don't have the time, don't have the resources. It will change my whole life. *"Maybe one day, but not now!"*

In this early stage, you have a decision to make: abort, neglect, or nurture the vision:

> **Abort** - You speak death to your vision through negative words, doubt, and unbelief. "Death and life are in the power of the tongue" (Prov. 18:21).
>
> **Neglect** - You disregard your "prenatal" care, resulting in underdeveloped, incomplete, or unachieved goals. Attention is given only during periods of hype. The vision may be birthed, but it is immature and unable to sustain itself. Or, it may be birthed into an environment that is not ready to help it to thrive and succeed.
>
> **Nurture** - You choose carefully what you speak, see, think, and hear. You sustain the vision through positive affirmations of faith enriched with God's Word. You are selective about the books you read, people you converse with, TV and radio programs you tune into. You speak life and health to your vision.

Choose Life

I hadn't seen my friend Belinda, a single mom, in years, so it was exciting to hear that she had married the man of her dreams. But shortly after the marriage he became unemployed, ran up the credit card debt, and left her. As hard as it would be to clean up her finances while raising the children from her previous marriage, she learned she was pregnant. What should she do? Her mother greatly protested the idea of adding another child to her single-parent household, as did most of her friends. After praying about it, she had a dream.

The Lord told Belinda that the baby's name was Isaiah. He said nothing more to influence her decision. But knowing that the Lord had already called her child by name, she advised the family of her decision. She called everyone, including her mother, and declared, "I'm going to have this baby." Before they could react she added, "I need to know if I should put you on the list of people who will support me in my decision. During the pregnancy, I won't be talking to anyone who's not on the list."

I'm sure those doubters were thinking, "Oh no she di-in't!"

Oh, but she did!

Prepare the Nursery *(That Baby's Coming!)*

Your life is pregnant with purpose! As the Lord reveals more, the vision increases and grows inside you until it pains you so much you are about to burst.

> Your life is pregnant with purpose!

"Therefore say unto them, Thus saith the Lord GOD; There shall none of my words be prolonged any more, but the word which I have spoken shall be done, saith the Lord GOD."

(Ezek. 12:28)

Your labor is not in vain. A holy thing shall be born of thee! *Are you making room for your blessing?* Preparing the nursery requires that you create an atmosphere around you to assure that the vision is birthed into a healthy environment. Get excited and *throw yourself a "Vision Shower"* as you prepare for this divine moment.

Use the Nursery Preparation Checklist:

Clean House – Make room for the promise! De-clutter your life of the former things; the way you used to live, who and what surrounded you, how you spend your time. Remove distractions and contentious people who are adverse to the vision. Something new and exciting is coming!

Visuals - Post photos, Scriptures or other visuals of what the vision will look like when it matures.

Godparents - Make a list of faith-filled people who will help to sustain the vision.

Library - Every nursery needs story hour items like books and CDs that will impart wisdom for the journey.

Parental Support Groups - Attend conferences and meetings with others who are serious about being good stewards and caretakers of what God has brought forth in their lives.

Prepare and make room for your promise, because surely at the appointed time, the vision will manifest. You will give birth to the greatest accomplishment you've ever achieved and beyond what you imagined.

Wanted: Birthing Coach

Though the enemy may give the command to kill your vision, God may send a midwife to help keep your vision alive. A midwife coaches you through the process of pregnancy and childbirth, reminding you to stay focused on the important things that will bring about an "expected end" (Jer. 29:11). .

Midwives are trained in the importance of focus and bonding. In fact, they command the mother to focus, because this is especially critical to the birthing process. If the mother is drifting or fading out, it requires commanding her to stay with it, with all the force and participation she can muster.

> *"...and Rachel travailed, and she had hard labour. And it came to pass, when she was in hard labour, that the midwife said unto her, "Fear not; thou shalt have this son also."*
>
> (Gen. 35:16-1)

It is important to connect with someone who can help you stay focused and keep your heart from fear. Rachel's midwife commanded her, "Don't be afraid, because this one also is a son for you!" She coached her to focus on what was coming—her son, her future!

Having children was Rachel's long time dream and desire. Though she was near to death, the mid-wife helped her not only to birth a dream, but a legacy that lives to this day.

What is your life-long dream?

Connect with someone who will help you believe and not fear that this vision is for you!

God's Goodness On Parade

Everybody loves a parade. My favorite parade took place on Mount Sinai when the Lord told Moses, "I will make all my goodness pass before you" (Ex. 33:19). He was saying, "I will do marvels such as have never been seen. Come, let me show you your future, all the abundant good that's going to come upon you just because you asked to be in my presence."

Just as Moses had a vision of things to come, the Lord wants to reveal his plans for us, such as have never been seen.

> *"But as it is written, Eye hath not seen, nor ear heard, neither have entered into the heart of man, the things which God hath prepared for them that love Him. But God hath revealed them to us by His Spirit: for the Spirit searcheth all things, yea, the deep things of God."*
>
> (1 Cor. 2:9, 10)

This parade is for an audience of one – you!

Can It Live Again?

Even where there has been success, the vision can diminish, become stale, or regress if someone doesn't keep it alive. It's like driving through a ghost town or an abandoned amusement park. You can almost hear the echoes of times gone by and imagine it in its former state.

Prophesy to your vision! Just like Ezekiel in the valley of dry bones, the Lord can resurrect your vision and bring it back to life (see Ezek. 37:1-14). When things become stagnant, God will send a visionary. Someone with new ideas and a fresh anointing. Still, the vision is your responsibility. Never entrust the vision God has given you to someone else.

The road can be long with winding paths, blind curves, and unforgiving terrain. Do not grow weary. *Keep the dream inside alive:*

- Confess daily what you expect to come to pass.
- Surround yourself with other dreamers as a source of inspiration.
- Keep it before your eyes as a visual. Post pictures or Scriptures in your view.
- Make note of accomplishments. Celebrate small successes.
- Appreciate and study other achievers, those who have birthed great visions.

Keep the dream inside alive:

May each vision and every one of the dreams you have conceived be birthed into the full manifestation of His glory!

Well, you do have that pen and paper ready, don't you?

Letter to My Future

It's time to write your third and final letter.

In this letter you are prophesying to your future. Using the *"Letter to my Future" template at the end of the chapter,* describe what you want your future to look like. Describe the kind of person you will be. You have dreamed about it; you have prayed about it. Now call those things that be not as though they were (Rom. 4:17).

Make a copy. This time you won't be giving a second copy to another person. You will seal it away in a time capsule, or something of the sort, to be opened a few years from now.

Set a timely reminder on your computer's electronic calendar. Imagine the excitement of receiving a message about your future a few years from now.

Hold a party for the unsealing of a message from the past!

Reflections Of The Journey

- God's vision for you will be beyond what you are humanly capable of accomplishing.

- Don't wish, make a list! Put it in writing. Bring it out of the unseen into the natural realm.

- Vision is long term. If you can get it all done tomorrow, it isn't vision.

- As soon as you commit your vision to paper you can expect two things: strategy and adversity will be your constant companions. Know them well.

- If the dream in your heart is from God, it will stay in your heart until it comes to fruition.

- Create an atmosphere around you to assure that the vision is birthed into a healthy environment.

- You are not just pursuing a goal, you are birthing a promise!

The Journey Continues . . .

Exercise

Your 60 Second Commercial

How do you envision your dream? You should be able to summarize it at any given time in 60 seconds or less:

_____

_____

To detect vision loss or vision blindness – **Take *The Vision Test!***

The Vision Test

Does your vision *(10 points for every "Yes")*:

_____ Utilize your gifts and talents?

_____ Help people?

_____ Seem bigger than you?

_____ Promote the Kingdom of God, not exalt darkness?

_____ Require you to connect with others?

_____ Keep coming back to you?

_____ Keep you coming back to God?

_____ **TOTAL**

How'd you do?

_____ (10 – 20) Completely Out of Focus

_____ (30 – 50) Becoming Clearer

_____ (60 – 70) Sharp!

Letter To My Future

It's time to write your third and final letter. *In this letter you are to prophesy to your future!* Describe what you want it to look like. Describe the kind of person *you* will be. Make a copy and seal it away in a time capsule, or something of the sort, to be opened a few years from now. At the appointed time, hold a party for the unsealing of a message from the past!

_____

_____

_____

_____

_____

_____

_____

_____

_____

_____

_____

_____

_____

_____

_____   _____
Signature   Date

"Good is The Enemy of Great."

– Jim Collins

Chapter 13
Your Assignment

Do you remember when your parents sent you to the store with a list of items to be purchased? In our small hometown, we could walk to the store. But once we got there we'd sometimes get distracted by all the goodies that lined the shelves, or start chatting with a friend and forget all about the list. And sometimes even lose it. Mom would hear us come through the front door and yell from upstairs, "Did you get everything I sent you for?" She'd be descending the stairs, reaching for the grocery bags, and at the same time naming things that should be inside. Just then you'd realize that you forgot something on the list. Grandma would actually pin the list to your shirt. No excuses.

I somehow envision God asking something similar of us when we reach the gates of Heaven. "Did you do all that I sent you to do?"

Gulp. Oh sure, we've been busy with lots of things, even good things. But the enemy of great is good. Had we done as He instructed, we would have accomplished all that we were sent for. If you're supposed to be volunteering as a mentor to a youngster on the east side of town every Friday at

> That good thing may not necessarily be the God thing for your life.

2:00, what are you doing picking up cans with your recycling club on the west side of town? Every unmet need is an opportunity. But every good opportunity is not necessarily a God-given opportunity.

You have an assignment in the earth. Something you were uniquely created, designed, and equipped to do. It is your lifelong destiny. But it can get lost in a busy world of tasks, activities, and even good deeds.

That good thing may not necessarily be the God thing for your life.

Did you know that God differentiates between promises birthed in the Spirit and those produced by our flesh? In Genesis 22, God referenced Isaac as Abraham's "only son." When it was time to get down to business, He did not even acknowledge Ishmael, the son Abraham and Sarah had conspired together to produce outside of the will of God. And although God provided for Ishmael, it was Isaac that He blessed and carried His covenant promises through to generations.

Stay in the Spirit!

"When I Say No, I Feel Guilty" (sign up today)

A former boss whom I didn't think even noticed me, signed me up for a class because she saw me running here and there trying to be all things to all people: clients, church, family and friends. It seemed everyone was living my life but me.

The class, "When I Say No I Feel Guilty" set me free as I gave myself permission to establish boundaries in my life.

I was no longer ripping and running from place to place. Knowing that God doesn't assign me to every person or even the same person on a daily basis, I can focus on whatever or to whomever He directs my attention.

But be prepared, especially if you're normally viewed as an easygoing person. People will be shocked when you set boundaries and say no. Often that same person you went out of your way for yesterday or made a lifetime of sacrifices for, will label you as inflexible, selfish, or inconsiderate because you refused them today. (And for me, that took some getting used to.)

Knowing the assignment in your life and sticking to it works well on the job too. Often, when we look back and review the events of the day, it becomes very clear what was meaningful and important vs. what was routine or simply distracting. So it may help to start with the end in mind. What must be accomplished by day's end? Begin with prayer for godly wisdom on how to prioritize tasks. Take inventory at the end of the day. Ask, who have I pleased most, God or man? I sleep much better knowing I completed something according to God's plan.

Somehow we've come to think that if the assignment wasn't physically or mentally exhausting, it wasn't from God. We can't seem to fathom that the most meaningful thing God may want us to do in a day is to pray for someone, or give something. His yoke is easy and his burden is light. I find that if I do the things God asks of me first, the rest will come easy. If I take care of His business, He takes care of mine.

Speaking of sleeping, your God-given assignment at times may be to rest. When we don't have required rest, our bodies protest and we bear the consequences of sickness and disease. God knows when we are weary and sometimes even appoints a season of rest. "He maketh me to lie down in green pastures" (Ps. 23: 2). I'm so used to being on the go that I find it strange when I have several days of nothing to do. But I have learned that what usually follows is something that will require much of me, often over an extended period of time. Appreciate the opportunity to rest whenever you can get it. You'll need it for the journey ahead.

I am not the same person in the natural as I am in the Spirit, flowing in purpose. It's amazing the things I cannot do of myself, but when I apply purpose to it, I can rise up and excel. A challenge may seem to overwhelm me, but when I see purpose in it, suddenly it's no longer I, but the Christ that lives in me. Suddenly, I can achieve!

Master Your Day - *Rock Your World!*

So how do we remain centered on our assignment? *Take control of your world each morning by releasing positive confession into your atmosphere*; put faith into action with good planning and execution; lean not unto your understanding, but rely on godly wisdom; and maintain absolute, unbendable, resolute focus! Consistency in these five areas will *guarantee* you the realization that you're a lot more in control of your life than you thought. Let's examine each of these in a little more detail.

1. *Confession*

Speech is spiritual. What we say with our mouth repeatedly conditions our brain to think toward that end, good or bad. Positive affirmations of faith enriched with God's word are necessary because the Bible says that what we have results from what we say (see Mark 11:23). What you nourish the vision with determines what it will produce. *If bad things keep happening to your good intentions, it's because of what you are speaking over your situation, or allowing others to.*

> Good or bad, your tongue is writing your life's story.

Good or bad, your tongue is writing your life's story. "My tongue is the pen of a ready writer." (Ps. 45:1). God created His world by speaking it into existence. We are created in His image and likeness, such that death and life are also in the power of our tongue (Prov. 18:21). Whatever you have been speaking into your own life over the past several weeks, months, and years is what you have today. What have you been saying? "I'm so broke. I'm so fat. I'm so sick. I'll never achieve anything, never be more than what I am. I'm a complete failure!" Whatever your ears hear, your heart receives, your brain agrees, and everything in your life begins to align itself with that mission statement.

> *"You have been trapped by what you said, ensnared by the words of your mouth."*
>
> (Prov. 6:2, NIV)

Wow.

Stop owning things that aren't yours, such as "my" arthritis, "my" tumor, etc. There's a difference between acknowledging things that occur in your life and giving power to them through ownership. So when you wonder, or even complain about why things haven't changed or gotten any better for you, the answer is that you've been speaking one thing and expecting another!

> You've been speaking one thing and expecting another!

Music is powerful. Singing the lyrics of songs is a form of confession. Don't just sing along because a song has a good beat or melody. Be mindful of the words. If you are singing along, you agree!

Find Scriptures that uplift, encourage, and support the vision God has given you. Share them with those who are praying with you, to assure that everyone is in agreement.

Once during a time when my niece lived with me, she said, "Auntie, the Lord told me in prayer that there is something you do every morning that pleases Him. What is it?"

I thought a minute. (Uh, get up in the morning? Lord knows I've never been a morning person!) Then it dawned on me. My daily confession. I shared with her that *each morning I speak over myself what the Word of God has already said about me*. I confess that I am blessed, healed, wise, and prosperous. That I walk in truth, peace, and love. I say that I am called to bless others and begin to call in favor, open doors and promises that will enable me to accomplish the things God has appointed me to do. I declare that I shall cover the earth with His glory, His power, and His love. What a great way to start the day!

What say you?

2. Wisdom (Brings Rewards)

Information alone will not suffice. Information is raw material. Wisdom makes it meaningful and applicable for your life. Wisdom sparks creativity and brings you new and clever ideas and inventions.

> "I, wisdom dwell with prudence, and find out knowledge of witty inventions."
>
> (Prov. 8:12)

God has made wisdom available to us in abundant supply (see James 1:5) and for good reason. The ability to obtain riches is fruitless if you can't hold on to it. Notice how God pairs riches with wisdom:

> *"Riches and honour are with me (wisdom); yea durable (longlasting) riches and righteousness."*
>
> (Prov. 8:18)

Sweet! Not only will you have the power and creativity to get wealth, but the wisdom to keep it. Wisdom is one of God's most under-utilized resources. We pray for increase in faith, finances, health, and peace, but how often do you hear someone say they are seeking God diligently for wisdom? We'd be a lot farther down the road if we learned to seek more wisdom and fewer things.

So many times, the new department head would give an assignment that baffled the whole staff. She naturally excelled in the kind of high level thinking that left us all in the dust. I wasn't quite sure what she wanted, but knew I had to produce! I began to pray daily for wisdom before I walked into my office. I asked God to search my boss' mind and heart to discern exactly what results she wanted and needed for our department. I asked for *"uncommon wisdom, creativity, and witty inventions"* to meet that need. I was amazed. So was she! She was so pleased with my project management that she rewarded me publicly and privately. She nicknamed me the "Smooth Operator." At a staff meeting, my co-workers joined in and honored me by calling me "Queen," for the rest of the day.

I did not pray for the rewards; they came with wisdom!

It's a packaged deal.

3. Planning

By personal experience, I find that if I'm disorganized, I am paralyzed. I simply cannot function. I find myself moving stacks of paper around my desk. *The more organized I am, the more productive I am.*

Excellence is not birthed out of chaos, but line upon line, precept upon precept. Vision is the big picture, but behind the scenes you will have to commit to a step-by-step, sometimes tedious process. Planning is the next critical step, complete with timelines of what needs to be accomplished when and by whom. An action plan will give you direction and keep you motivated. It must be well thought out and well organized.

A word of caution: expect your plan to be outdated the day after you finish it. If your vision is forward moving, you will continue to get fresh ideas. Keep up with it and run with it.

Good planning can turn your problems into possibilities!

> Good planning can turn your problems into possibilities!

4. Executing

Are you "all talk"?

Lots of people talk a good game, but a great many do not follow through on their plans. Once, as I was comparing candidates I had interviewed for my new assistant's position, the head of our department made a noteworthy statement: "I'd rather have an average employee who had consistent follow-through than one who was brilliant and undependable." In other words:

> *"What you do in your finest hour is who you could be. What you do consistently is who you really are."*
> -- Pastor G.F. Watkins, PowerHouse Church

People must be able to value your word. It's more important than you think. Who would you trust your business to, a person who delivers on time consistently? Or someone you have to constantly track down and pray they meet your deadlines? Active faith is follow-through and is an essential key to success.

Are your dreams faltering? No matter how many inspirational books you read, or motivational seminars you attend, unless you fully and consistently commit to a plan of action you will continuously experience remorse over unachieved dreams and goals. In other words:

Inspiration without demonstration leads to frustration!

Failure to communicate the vision effectively is equally fatal. Just because you click "Send" on your email doesn't mean you effectively communicated.

> Inspiration without demonstration leads to frustration!

You can have the greatest vision, but not know how to deliver it into the hands of the people who will execute and carry it out. Left to each individual's interpretation, it causes di-vision. *If the right people are in place and they aren't running with your vision, either it isn't clear, or it isn't time.*

"And make it plain (clear, simple) …that he may run who reads it."

Moses had the vision, but the fight was in Joshua! He ran with the vision God had begun in Moses. Likewise, much of David's plans were manifested through the wisdom of his son, Solomon. At the appointed time, the Lord will raise up Joshuas and Solomons in your midst to bring the fullness of your vision to pass.

5. Focus

I saved focus for last because distractions are the granddaddy of all reasons our plans fail. Distractions slow you down. Always be aware that distractions sometimes mask themselves as opportunities. Remember, every good thing is not necessarily the God thing for you at this time. (Double-click on that!) Stay on assignment. Stay in prayer.

> Distractions sometimes mask themselves as opportunities

If this is your challenge area, pray for the ability to discern your true assignment daily. The ability to focus is a great asset and can give you the competitive advantage. *Everyone can dream, but success comes to those who stay on assignment.*

Discovering Daily Purpose - Living in the Moment

We can never be fulfilled if we are constantly looking for what's beyond the bend. What set me free was discovering daily purpose and God-given assignments.

It's exciting to know that God's plan for you tomorrow may be quite different from the one in place today. So you can see why you can't allow yourself to get stuck. Today's purpose is freshly fallen manna. Yesterday's purpose is stale bread.

Make a decision to excel in something *today*.

Your Assignment

Living "in the moment" is an area I had trouble in. If all you ever focus on is the next step, you will always be disappointed. Look around and appreciate what and who is in your life today. It may not be there tomorrow. Tomorrow these will be the good old days. Learn to live in the moment. Milk it for all it's worth.

> This moment controls the next moment.

Think to yourself: "This moment controls the next moment." That is why it deserves your respect. Success is a journey. It's not about an event, but the process. What's different about you now than when you started out? What did you learn? How did you change?

Hear ye: the process of growing, giving back, learning, and teaching is the purpose of the journey, not a single destination in itself.

Adopt as your mantra, *"I will walk in purpose today!"*

What Is Your Assignment (For Today)?

There is a secret to discovering your assignment on earth. *It is hidden in your daily environment.* If you think of your assignment as a one-and-done lifetime event, you will miss it. It is a day by day discovery.

Now I ask daily, Lord "what" is your assignment for me today? And Lord, "who" is your assignment for me today? *Friend, this is one of the most powerful prayers you can ever pray!* You will begin to "encounter" people, rather than have casual conversations in passing. Suddenly the Lord will shine a spotlight on something that is spoken, and you will think, "Aha, this is my assignment for today." It won't happen with everyone (and usually not when you think it would), but when it does you will be very much aware of His presence and your part in the assignment. Nothing else in the day will matter, because you will sense how pleased God is that you asked and allowed Him to use you in ways He deemed important. No longer will you balk at things that unexpectedly interrupt your day. Instead you'll pause to consider – *Could this be my assignment for today?*

> Ask daily, Lord "what" is your assignment for me today?

As you do this consistently, you'll soon begin to see a pattern in the ways God uses you. *He reveals your lifelong assignment on earth through your daily interactions.*

> He reveals your lifelong assignment on earth through your daily interactions.

The day you begin to pray that powerful prayer you'll become Heaven's "secret agent". Each morning you'll check in saying, "Lord, what is my assignment for today?" And in response He'll say, "This is your mission for today, if you choose to accept it." That ought to make you excited about waking up each morning!

Your assignment may require you to:

- Meet someone at a specific point of need
- Give time, money, or talent to another's work
- Learn something valuable that will impact a future assignment
- Intercede for a specific person or cause
- Build yourself up in the Spirit so that you will be prepared for the enemy's attack
- Encourage a weary heart
- Rest

A dear friend was recovering from a complicated surgical procedure in Houston. At the same time, the pressure was on to sell the family home in Phoenix, since they were relocating to New Mexico. In her extended family, she was the one always directing life like a symphony. They were missing that element from their lives, and she was feeling the pressure to "get well soon." We bustled through the airport with three kids in tow, arriving in Phoenix late that evening. Everyone was exhausted, so no work got done on day one.

I had come along with the intention of packing up the house, but seemed to keep getting sidetracked. People of purpose don't feel comfortable when the assignment at hand is getting away from them. In another day and a half I would be leaving, not having performed my duties.

Your Assignment

After a day of running errands, I figured this was a good time for me and the kids to get started on packing. Just then, my friend asked if I would change her bandages, take her to the bank, and fix her hair. She hadn't been able to get to the salon since the surgery. About that time, it dawned on me: My assignment was not to pack her house. My assignment was to minister to *her*!

Here's another example: One morning, I wasn't feeling well but went to work anyway. Later in the day, I realized I hadn't encountered anyone or anything that stood out. I began to wonder if I'd missed it. So, about 3:00, I inquired of the Lord, to which He replied, "You were your assignment for today. You were supposed to take care of *you*."

I'm recognizing my assignment much quicker than I used to. Years ago, my assistant and I shared an office. Though it seemed we just busied ourselves unendingly with the tasks at hand, the note she sent when she left the company revealed much more:

> *... just wanted to say "thank you" for your support and friendship over the years. I mean, honestly, you had a huge impact on my life while working together (and even now!) and I know that God put us together so I could get that experience. Between you answering all my child-like questions about the bible and Jesus to being such an incredible source of strength for me, I can't thank you enough.*
>
> *I still tell people today that if it weren't for you and your sharing God's love (and your own!) with me, I don't know that I could have gotten through the difficult times I had, moving on, etc. I know that certain people are put in our lives to make a difference and I truly believe that you were put in mine... You are such an amazing woman and I just wanted to say thank you for everything that you have done for me - whether you knew you were doing it or not!*

She was my assignment! (*Duh*)

Reflections Of The Journey

- Take control of your world each morning by releasing positive confession into your atmosphere.

- Every good thing is not necessarily the "God thing" for you at this time.

- Inspiration without demonstration leads to frustration.

- Distractions sometimes mask themselves as opportunities.

- Adopt as your mantra, "I will walk in purpose today!"

- Ask daily, Lord "what" is your assignment for me today? And Lord, "who" is your assignment for me today?

- Tell yourself, "This moment, controls the next moment."

The Journey Continues . . .

Exercise

Your Assignment

The secret to discovering your assignment on earth is hidden in your daily environment.

List a couple of *"good" things* you do for others on a regular basis:

Name *something* you were recently asked to do that you found difficult to say no to:

Name *someone* that you regularly find it difficult to say no to:

Reflect for a moment on each of the above. Ask God to show you if <u>any</u> of these *good things* (no sacred cows!) may be keeping you from *God-things* (thou shalt have no other gods before Him).

In order to master your day, identify which of the following area(s) you seem to have the most difficulty in. Even better, ask a friend, spouse, or co-worker for input!

- ☐ *Confession* – Speaking positively about your situation.
- ☐ *Wisdom* – Seeking God for wisdom and applying it to daily challenges.
- ☐ *Planning* – Approaching your goals in a well thought out and strategic way.
- ☐ *Executing* – Keeping your word, and consistently following through with results.
- ☐ *Focus* – Avoiding distractions and staying on assignment.

Identify a scripture that you will speak into the atmosphere each morning that aligns with what the Word of God says about you or your circumstances:

What will you ask of the Lord *daily* in regards to seeking your assignment?

Chapter 14
Return to the Garden

Mystery of the Garden

Once upon a time there existed a place on earth of perfect peace and fullness. No death, no lack, no sickness. Life in the Garden of Eden was a place of love and intimacy with the Father. God's original plan was to share this special place with generations of His beloved creation. But through an act of disobedience, paradise was lost. The first man, Adam, died a spiritual death that resulted in separation from God. Through Adam, sin and death was passed upon all mankind.

Is it any wonder that the last stop on Earth for Jesus before Calvary was the garden? He agonized there because we lost it there. But Calvary would buy it all back for us.

Back to the Future

If one act of disobedience could lose it all, one sovereign act of obedience could get it all back. Jesus was obedient to the cross. And on the cross He said "Today you will be with me in paradise." He gave it back to us! The veil that separated man and holy God was rent in two and the door was opened, giving us legal access back to the garden. We would once again know life eternal, abundance, and intimacy with the Father. We would have victory over death, sin, lack, and disease, just like in the garden. We could once again fulfill God's original plan for His children to subdue the earth and have dominion.

Enter the Garden

Our individual obedience and acceptance of the cross is our ticket back inside the garden. Jesus said "I AM the door." Each of us must make the choice to enter in through that door. That's it, just one act of obedience – accepting the benefits of the cross and all the love your heart can stand!

The moment you receive salvation through the cross, you walk through the door. But as phenomenal as that is, it is sad that many Christians go only that far. They hang out just inside the door, never exploring the full benefits of the garden made available through the cross.

Enter in!

Most importantly, Christ's obedience restored the relationship between God and man. Not since Adam's fall did we as the human race (the creature), commune with God (the Creator). Only select, Old Testament priests and prophets had that privilege. Now direct communication with God through Jesus Christ is available to "whosoever will." Let him come through prayer. Let him *return to the garden and share intimacy with God* through His Holy Spirit, a special gift sent from the Father to dwell within us. *This time, instead of placing man in the garden, He places the garden in man!*

Perhaps you are thinking there is more God could be doing instead of talking to you. But it is His greatest pleasure! He has promised to be with us until the end. Day and night, mid-day and midnight, He will never leave us alone.

There is not a more awesome experience on this earth than supernatural communion with God through the Holy Spirit!

I pray you will visit the garden often on your journey. He will always meet you there.

A Night to Remember

During my junior year in college I met a graduate student by the name of William, who identified himself as a Christian. It seemed every time I entered the cafeteria, he'd be sitting all alone at a long table. We'd have in-depth conversations about salvation, and one day he asked me if I was familiar with speaking in tongues. I was, but it wasn't a part of my religious experience. He could not have known this, but I had been praying in my dorm room for God to give me this heavenly language. For some reason, pride I guess, I did not share this with William. In fact, I maintained that it wasn't a necessary part of the believer's walk. But William enticed me by sharing the affect his prayer language had on his prayer life. He compared this awesome communication to God speaking with the angels in His presence.

I wanted it!

My hunger for the Lord intensified, and I began to seek Him earnestly:

> *"I will rise now, and go about the city in the streets, and in the broad ways I will seek him whom my soul loveth: I sought him, but I found him not. The watchmen that go about the city found me: to whom I said, Saw ye him whom my soul loveth? It was but a little that I passed from them, but I found him whom my soul loveth: I held him, and would not let him go..."*
>
> (Song of Sol. 3:2-4)

I sang in a campus choir with friends from surrounding universities, and one day they invited me to join them at an off-campus church service. They revealed that the previous week they had all been baptized there and filled with the Holy Spirit, evidenced by speaking in other tongues. *I was jealous.* The next Sunday I joined them. When the altar call came, I was baptized. I spent the next few hours on my knees, surrounded by church mothers telling me to "Keep on saying Jesus; Now say Hallelujah; Hold on, sister; Now let it go!" I would feel a stirring within, but to tell you the truth, I couldn't keep my mind on what was happening. Honestly, I was thinking about how all this might drastically change my life, and wasn't sure I was ready for it. Then something interesting happened.

Two young girls, about eleven years old, knocked on the door. I heard the sisters scolding them for interrupting God's work. Next thing I knew, they were kneeling next to me, receiving the same instructions I had. Within a few moments time, one little girl was speaking in tongues. A few moments later, both girls were rejoicing in the Spirit with tears streaming down their little faces.

That did something for me. I knew I had to come to Christ as a little child, totally trusting Him. I lifted my hands and told the Lord that I surrendered my *whole* life to him. I began to feel that stirring within again, but this time I decided to yield to it. I took a deep breath and out came something wonderful, something I'd never heard before. It was just one word that phonetically sounded like "Ru-wah." But I was so proud of my little word, I just kept repeating it. I was not only amazed, but felt truly special. The Holy Spirit Himself was moving inside of me. Me! It was so exciting, even electrifying. I threw my hands up in jubilation.

Late that night as I exited the prayer room, a distinguished, older man waited at the top of the stairs, his coat and hat in hand. I later learned he was the pastor. No matter how long it took, Bishop Thomas would not go home until all the babies emerged from that delivery room, full of the Spirit!

I couldn't wait to tell William. But mostly, I couldn't wait to get back to my dorm room, away from the church and the excitement of the people who had been cheering me on. I wanted to know if it was real. I figured that if Jesus showed up in my dorm room, just as He had at church, then it was real. Well, I called, and He came. Night after night, I sat on the side of my bed and enjoyed my new experience, hearing it flow out of my mouth repeatedly and with such fervor! I didn't even care that it didn't make sense to me. I looked forward to it each night. I wept with my hands lifted saying, "Ruwah! Ruwah! Ruwah!" I was, however, disappointed that I only had one word in my spiritual vocabulary. But I believed God for more words and before long I was flowing in a beautiful heavenly language. I wanted Him. I sought Him. And *I found Him in the Garden.*

What could be more awesome? Well, many years later while reading the book *They Speak with Other Tongues* written by a reporter named John L. Sherrill, something stood out on the pages. It was the mention that the Hebrew word for spirit is Ruah or Ruach (same pronunciation as my little word Ruwah). Also meaning: *wind, breath of God, voice of God!*

I had no idea what I was saying back then.

It's a moment that still makes me cry, "Oh my gosh!" while fanning tears.

He Is...

Master Teacher

It was like I had a new Bible. In my quest for truth, I had previously made a commitment to read the entire Old and New Testament. But I had been reading with no understanding. That changed dramatically once I received the Holy Spirit.

He began to show me how different passages of Scripture related to one another. And I began to see the storyline, the meaning or message God was intending to get across. But I was most excited when *the Master Teacher began to show me how Scripture applied to my own life.* Not only did the black and white pages seem to come to life, but certain verses now seemed to be illuminated, as if to say, "This is for you today" (the *Logos* became *rhema*). That was my cue to study more about a particular Scripture. Many times I heard the same Scripture the Lord had given me in my study time come right across the pulpit the next Sunday morning.

Salvation secures for us life eternal, but the Holy Spirit empowers us to walk this life in victory.

> Salvation secures for us life eternal, but the Holy Spirit empowers us to walk this life in victory.

Discerner of Truth

> Jesus spoke with great enthusiasm about the Spirit of Truth.

Jesus spoke with great enthusiasm about the Spirit of Truth, the comforter that would come to live within us once He returned to Heaven. "He will guide you into all truth," Jesus said.

The Holy Spirit helps us discern truth from deception, and righteousness from sin.

Intercessor

Do you ever not know how or what to pray about a situation? Pray in the Spirit! Because according to Romans 8:26-27, *when we don't know what to pray, Holy Spirit makes intercession for us.* He searches our hearts and knows the mind of God. Then He intercedes for us according to the will of God. What a great benefit!

So, what exactly is it that we utter when we are praying in the Holy Ghost? You utter words you can't find to express in your human language. You utter words of prayer and of the highest praise. You utter words that you don't have strength within yourself to pray, words that edify and build up your faith. And you utter words that align with the Word of God and the perfect will of God, so that you don't ask "amiss."

Comforter

"I go unto my Father," Jesus said to His disciples before he was crucified. But He also wanted to assure them that in some way, He would still be with them:

> *"And I will pray the Father, and he shall give you another Comforter, that he may abide with you forever; Even the Spirit of truth; whom the world cannot receive, because it seeth him not, neither knoweth him: but ye know him; for he dwelleth in you, and shall be in you. I will not leave you comfortless: I will come to you."*
>
> (John 14: 16-18)

Some called Jesus teacher, some healer, some deliverer. Be comforted in the fact that everything Jesus was in the flesh is still available to us through the Holy Spirit.

Wonderful Counselor

> *"Whether you turn to the right or to the left, your ears will hear a voice behind you saying 'This is the way; walk in it."*
>
> (Isa. 30:21, NIV)

You could benefit from a little divine counsel and direction, couldn't you?

When faced with a task I don't quite understand, I practice something I learned from Dr. Mike Murdock; I call upon the Lord for uncommon wisdom, creativity, and witty inventions (Prov. 8:12; Eph. 3:20). God knows something you don't know or can't see with human eyes. *He wants to help you in everything you do, not just "spiritual" matters.*

Isn't it good to know that you don't have to walk alone or try to figure out life on your own?

Transformer

The Holy Spirit draws us to salvation. His next assignment is to transform us, to strengthen and equip us so we can walk in the Spirit.

> *"…wait for the promise of the Father, which, saith He, ye have heard of Me. But ye shall receive power after that the Holy Ghost is come upon you."*
>
> (Acts 1:4, 8)

We may mean well when we say we want to be changed. But sometimes we don't really know how to go about it. You may think everything is okay and that your heart is right, but don't rely on self. Ask the Lord to search your heart and identify areas of needed change. Do it daily.

We must yield to the Holy Spirit, allowing Him to "net-op" in and control the mouse.

He then works undercover, like a stealth undetected, changing your heart, renewing your mind, and downloading the mind of Christ into your human program. Little by little, you will begin to manifest the ability to love someone you couldn't love before, do things you couldn't do before, see things differently. This kind of transformation requires the power of a divine love.

> This kind of transformation requires the power of a divine love.

There are times when we desire to achieve something greater. But with our human limitations, it may seem out of reach or even impossible. Everything Jesus instructed us to go into all the world and do, He knew was impossible for us to do on our own. He said we should wait until we receive the promise of the Holy Spirit, and then we would have the power to be witnesses.

How else does a shy, bullied, sickly, fearful little girl with no voice of her own rise up to be a confident teacher, author, singer, and speaker?

He transformed me!

Don't you just love the Holy Spirit? Do you want the Holy Spirit?

Invite Him in!

Cry of the Heart

No matter what your lips are saying, God knows what's in your heart. He hears the cry of the heart. That's what prayer is. You can't fool God with insincere words and wrong motives.

The Bible says we must pray strategically, not frivolously.

When what is in your *heart* aligns with what's in God's Word, that's when you'll begin to pray with power.

When what is in your *mouth* aligns with God's Word, that's when you'll see God move mightily in your life.

> *"Out of the abundance of the heart the mouth speaks"*
> (Luke 6:45).

Search the Scriptures and fill your heart with an abundance of God's Word. The more you read and study God's Word, the more your mouth will confess it.

Although He is touched by your pain and sorrows, and most certainly aware of your needs, God does not move until your prayers and words earnestly and sincerely align with His Word. "Lord, I'm troubled" touches God, but when you add *"and your Word says,* you will keep me in perfect peace," now you're praying within the legal confines of the Word! *Angels of Heaven are on alert to recognize and act on the Word of God spoken in faith* no matter who is speaking it. They are now released to action. No need to speak a lot of lofty words. Just speak the language that all heaven understands: the Word of God. When you want an audience with the King, speak the King's language! Speak it aloud and doubt not. He will hear your heart's cry, move on behalf of His Word, and deliver you.

> When you want an audience with the King, speak the King's language!

The devil isn't all that bothered about people who pray. But he is greatly disturbed by those who know how to pray. In an urgent or stressful situation, my initial response is to pray out of my emotions. I have to remind myself, "Pray the Word, Pray the Word, Pray the Word."

7 Keys to Answered Prayer

1. Pray with right motives. Confess and release any unforgiveness or wrong doing.

2. Pray to the Father and petition Him in the name of Jesus (John 16:23). Honor Him with praise.

3. Pray the Word! Search the scriptures and find your promise. *Everything* we need is in the Word. (Just keep searching; it's in there!). Agree with that scripture daily.

4. Pray in the Spirit. Yield to the Holy Spirit and use your supernatural prayer language so that (according to 1 Cor. 14:2), you "speak to God" directly.

5. Proclaim your belief and trust in Him to move on your behalf.

6. Wait on the answer - with no restrictions on what *you* want the answer to be.
7. Thank Him often for the answer - before it even manifests.

Father Knows Best *(And the Answer Is)* ...

God's answers are:

- Yes.
- Wait.
- I've got something better for you!

Holy Spirit is not a courier or an order-taker. He doesn't just tell the Father that you want two of these and one of those, and then pass it through a drive-through window. *Holy Spirit intercedes, not just according to what you pray, but to return to you the perfect will of God for your life!* Many times the answer that comes might be foreign to you, something you have never experienced and therefore have no point of reference. In other words, you can't relate. The advice is simple. Get out of the box, move out of the way, and let God be God. Think about it, really. What pleasure would God have if He is restricted to moving only within the confines of *your* reality? What limitations would result?

Remember, Father knows best! The prayers you send up to Heaven cannot compare to what Heaven sends back to you.

God Is Speaking!

The answer may not reveal itself immediately and may come when you least expect it.

Picture yourself in your sacred prayer closet, on your knees, with just the right atmosphere. Sure seems like if God was going to speak, He'd speak now. Not! Days later, you may be cooking, brushing your teeth, or drifting off to sleep when the Holy Spirit announces, "You've got mail!" Or during Monday morning rush hour traffic while you are gathering your thoughts for the busy week ahead, God shows up and He wants to talk! If you want your answer, get on God's schedule. Be flexible. He may broadcast a single thought, instruction, or idea that you know was not your own. Your spirit tunes in and says, "That's it!" The answer may go off inside you like an explosion, or it may simply settle you.

> He is testing you to see if there are any other gods before Him in your life!

Get a picture in your mind of the upcoming week. What is the most important thing you have on your schedule? What activity, person, or event comes first in your life no matter what? Now cancel it. Can you? Will you set aside your hair appointment or sports activity when Almighty God summons you to a meeting? Your busiest times are often when He will show up and speak. *He is testing you to see if there are any other gods before Him in your life!*

God told Moses to take off his shoes so he could commune with him. What is it that He is asking you to take off, to get rid of or separate from so you can hear Him? It may actually be something you think is pleasing to God. But remember, the enemy of great is good! That activity, that person you allow to consume so much of your time may just be "noise" at the end of the day, distracting you from His voice.

God will send you messengers, but will you recognize them? When the Sunday sermon is speaking to your situation, will you write it down? When He lays you on someone's heart to give you a word from Him, will you interrupt that conversation and click over on two-way to take another call? When someone puts a book in your hand, or a teaching CD, will you dismiss it, or will you play that teaching CD as you would a music CD? Will you put it on repeat and listen over and over again? Each time you do, you will hear messages you didn't hear the first time.

And, He is speaking in your dreams:

> *"In a dream, in a vision of the night, when deep sleep falleth upon men, in slumberings upon the bed; then He openeth the ears of men, and sealeth their instruction."*
>
> (Job 33:15, 16)

Back to the Matrix

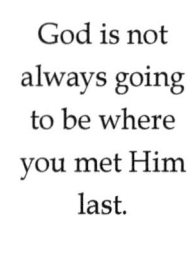

God is not always going to be where you met Him last.

In the movie *The Matrix*, when Neo needed a word, he returned to the apartment building where he first met The Oracle. But it was vacant. "Where are you?" he thought.

God is not always going to be where you met Him last.

This time, you may find Him through an act of obedience in giving, sowing, fasting or serving. He may speak to you through people you meet or certain places where you are sent. Sometimes, He's in your tears.

The Oracle was found on a park bench feeding birds. God is rarely where you expect Him to be.

My Secret Place

Before he was John the Revelator, John the beloved laid his head on Jesus' breast and heard the heartbeat of Jesus. I believe spiritually he "heard" what was in Jesus' heart for time and eternity.

Intimacy with God through worship, prayer, and meditation is essential to our faith. *He wants to share His heart!*

The tabernacle that the Lord instructed Moses to build for him consisted of three areas: the outer court, the inner court and the Holy of Holies. Later, the Lord revealed His true desire to dwell not in buildings, but in the hearts of men. *Your heart was designed to be the true tabernacle of God.* Sometimes the Lord will woo you into His inner courts. (You know, those times when you feel moved to pray but somehow keep busying yourself, turning up the TV?)

> *"My beloved spoke and said unto me, Rise up, my love, my fair one, and come away."*
>
> (Song 2:10)

> *I sleep, but my heart waketh: it is the voice of my beloved that knocketh, saying, open to me,"*
>
> (Song of Sol. 5:2)

> *"I am my beloved's and His desire is toward me."*
> (Song of Sol. 7:10)

Sometimes He desires to be wooed *by* us:

> *"... I found him whom my soul loveth: I held him and would not let him go..."*
> (Song of Sol. 3:4)

> *"While the king sitteth at his table, my spikenard sends forth the smell thereof."*
> (Song of Sol. 1:12)

> *"Let my prayer be sent forth before thee as incense; and the lifting of my hands as the evening sacrifice."*
> (Ps. 141:2)

> *"And the smoke of the incense, which came with the prayers of the saints, ascended up before God out of the angel's hand."*
> (Rev. 8:4)

We are His intimate sanctuary.

> We are His intimate sanctuary.

A Divine Encounter - Set The Atmosphere

There's no great mystery to getting to know God. Like any relationship, *getting to know Him simply involves spending time with Him.* Clear your mind. Get alone with God and listen inwardly for His still, small voice.

Nothing is conceived without intimacy. Give yourself to Him. This is His time. Enter into His gates with thanksgiving and into His courts with praise. Sing unto Him. Tell Him how good He is. Tell Him how great He's been in your life. Be thankful about ways He has specifically blessed you. Boast about how strong He is, how you believe He can do anything!

Who wouldn't stay in an atmosphere like that?

It is true that you can (and should) pray anytime, anywhere, staying in an attitude of prayer. But it is sometimes necessary to bow the knee and humble yourself physically in the presence of God. Dedicate a certain space in your home as the place where you meet and talk to God. Begin to worship God for no other reason than because God is, was, and always will be God. Acknowledge there is none like Him, nor shall there ever be.

For me, the sounds of nature heighten my worship experience. I turn on sound machines all around the house. I might have ocean waves in one room, and a fireplace with the pattering of gently falling rain in another. Near where I pray is a water fountain into which I add drops of aromatic oils like lavender, jasmine, frankincense, and myrrh. Lying prostrate before the Lord as David did also takes the worship experience to a whole new level.

In a dream, while going through a stressful time in my life, the Lord replayed this song throughout my sleep:

> *Stay at peace, Stacie*
> *Lay at my feet, Stacie*

God loves music. He loves you and inhabits your praise. He will show up. And He will share. "Call unto me, and I will answer you, and show you great and mighty things which you know not" (Jer. 33:3).

This is where it all happens. *The Secret Place is where He makes you to be all that He wants you to be inwardly before it ever manifests outwardly.* If you will spend time in the company of God, He will bring you into the company of those He has empowered to bless and make you great.

> The pathway you are seeking is hidden in God's presence.

> The Secret Place is where He makes you to be all that He wants you to be inwardly before it ever manifests outwardly.

The pathway you are seeking is hidden in God's presence. The promises you desire are hidden in God's presence. His prosperity is hidden in His presence. In His presence is His protection. In His presence is your portion—the fullness of joy!

In His presence, your prayers will have new wings!

Reflections Of The Journey

- Jesus spoke with great enthusiasm about the Spirit of Truth, the comforter that would come to live within us once He returned to Heaven.

- The Holy Spirit helps us discern truth from deception, and righteousness from sin.

- Speak the language that all Heaven understands, the Word of God.

- Father knows best. His answers to prayer are: Yes, Wait, or I've got something better!

- The Holy Spirit is not simply a courier or an order-taker. He intercedes on your behalf and returns to you the perfect will of God for your life!

- God is speaking in your dreams.

- The Secret Place is where God makes you to be all that He wants you to be inwardly before it ever manifests outwardly.

- The pathway you are seeking is hidden in God's presence.

The Journey Continues . . .

Chapter 15
The Sacred Cave

Have you ever found yourself in a situation where it seems like no one is there for you? Have you felt isolated, even in a crowd? Or maybe your job has relocated you far away from friends or relatives. Whatever the scenario, suddenly, you find yourself all alone.

Could it be you have been intentionally set apart from others? *Could it be that you are having a cave experience?*

God has set you alone and apart for a purpose.

Restoration By Isolation

But why a cave, you ask? Caves once functioned as ideal places to preserve things, to provide refuge, and to bury the dead. Some historical caves are regarded as sacred.

Here is where you gain wisdom and reassess your values. Here is where you permit your old ways to die and prepare for the new you. The purpose of your cave experience may be:

> Your cave experience will bring you restoration by isolation.

- to give you a place of refuge
- to preserve you
- to bury what is dead in your life

Your cave experience will bring you restoration by isolation. You will determine how long you must be there—weeks, months, or years. It all depends on your willingness to trust and obey.

Come with me to a hidden place, an unlikely treasure-filled fantasy land, "The Sacred Cave."

A Place of Refuge

The Bible describes a number of cave dwellers. David, while running from King Saul, lived in a cave. Obadiah hid a hundred prophets in a cave to save them from Jezebel. To escape the Midianites, the Israelites dwelt in caves. Elijah, who called fire down from Heaven, found himself in a strange and unexpected place, the cave.

Sometimes God leads you to a hiding place to conceal you so that trouble cannot find you. If you are finding it difficult to avoid distractions, *God may find it necessary to call you away to a place of solace where you can devote your thoughts to planning and developing strategy for the assignment He has for you.*

David, one of the greatest heroes of the Bible took refuge in a large underground cavern to conceal himself from Saul. Now a fugitive, David referred to his cave as being under the shadow of Gods wings. A place where he would make his refuge, "until these calamities be overpast." (Ps. 57:1). While in the cave, David had to think, pray, and strategize how he would win the victory.

Those who joined David in the cave were said to be "in distress, in debt, and discontented." But though they all began amid the gloomy shadows of the cavern, they gradually emerged into the open daylight and were referred to as mighty men. They had been transformed.

Expect to emerge from your cave into the daylight with your eyes opened and your spirit stronger and mightier than when you entered.

A Place of Preservation

Caves once functioned as places in which to store food, where cool temperatures year round helped preserve the harvest. To preserve means to:

- Keep or save from corruption, decomposition, or decay
- Set aside and apart
- Guard, keep secret to keep alive, maintain intact
- Reserve for personal or future use

Between 1947 and 1956, thousands of fragments of biblical and early Jewish documents were discovered in eleven caves near the site of Khirbet Qumran. They produced one of the most outstanding archeological discoveries of the twentieth century. A young Bedouin goat herdsman found some strange clay jars in caves near the valley of the Dead Sea. Inside the jars were some leather scrolls. It is believed that when a commune of monastic farmers saw the Romans invade the land, they put their cherished leather scrolls in the jars and hid them in the caves on the cliffs near the Dead Sea. When discovered, the "Dead Sea Scrolls" had been remarkably preserved over time.

Maybe you've been in an environment that is adverse to what God wants to do in your life. *A cave may be God's way of keeping you from corruption by setting you apart from bad influences in your life. Or it may protect you from your enemies, including those close to you that you don't recognize as enemies!*

If you've asked God for more depth, if you've sought Him for more revelation, you may have been drawn away to a place of seclusion where the Lord can speak into your right ear without concern that someone else may be speaking into the left.

Now and then we hear of someone who is on the move for God, but then seems to disappear. Just when you think he is never to be heard from again, he returns with fire and fervor. Where has he been? Shut in with Jesus!

Joseph's experiences included the pit and the prison. His family thought he was dead, but he had been shut away, preserved for future use, which was to save the Israelites from famine and death. He was kept secret to be kept alive. The prison preserved him. He was able to remain pure as long as he was kept apart from Potiphar's wife, who sought to defile him.

A Place to Bury the Dead

Abraham wept and mourned when he buried his beloved Sarah in the cave at Machpelah (Gen. 23:2, 19). Abraham's intent was to bury his dead "out of his sight." *There comes a time to put even those things we once loved out of sight.*

Perhaps without even realizing it, you may be giving life to those things, even if by thoughts words. Constantly replaying a mental picture of our past mistakes is not putting it out of sight. Talking repeatedly about the pain you experienced in a previous relationship is not keeping it out of sight.

Are you holding on to past hurts and memories? Are there habits, addictions, or unhealthy relationships you can't seem to let go of? Are you haunted by the shame or guilt of some former deed? Have you asked God for forgiveness or for healing from things that have occurred in your life? If so, *He has declared those things dead. You should too.*

Human beings are creatures of habit. It's difficult for us to let go. But your cave experience may be a result of the things in your life that need to be put to death. If you find that you are having difficulty, there may be a need for greater analysis. Autopsies are performed to examine, evaluate, and determine the cause of death. Before you can bury some things, you may need to determine what went wrong; otherwise you may repeat mistakes in the future. You could keep digging up the *same things,* reliving and re-enacting the *same problems,* only with *different people,* or in *different places.*

Echoing in the cavern walls are the cries of those who preceded you in burying their dead. Whatever the cost, in spite of the pain, they realized something – that *what you won't bury will someday bury you*. Bury *pride* in the cave. Bury *lies* in the cave. Failed relationships, bad business decisions—whatever is holding on to you and binding you to your past, is blinding you to your future. Leave it in the cave. Decide, once and for all, to put those things behind you and press toward the mark for the prize of the high calling.

> Whatever is holding on to you and binding you to your past, is blinding you to your future.

Peace to All Who Enter

Burying the dead or being hidden from your enemies may not be enough to give you an appreciation for what you are experiencing. You probably want to know more about that hidden fantasyland I mentioned earlier!

Follow me.

As we approach the mouth of the cave, we see that it is simply a cavity inside the earth. As we enter the cave, a brief science lesson is in order. Why and how was the cave formed?

The process of forming caves is very slow. It all begins with rain. As rain falls through the atmosphere and water and carbon dioxide seep through the cracks and crevices, it dissolves the soluble rock and forms cavities and channels.

Let's go deeper inside.

In many caves we find underground streams that grow into rivers, even lakes. When water drains away, the waterways turn into open cave tunnels, passages, and caverns.

Listen. (Drip … drip … drip)

Water drips constantly in caves. Because of the darkness in the cave, *your hearing grows keener.* Soon, information, instructions, and direction will be clearer to you. It was in a cave that Elijah heard the "still small voice" of the Lord (1 Kings 19:12). His voice can best be heard where the atmosphere is pure and clear. With keener ears you can even hear sacred music.

There is a stillness, a peace in the atmosphere. A peace that passes all understanding. You are drawn deeper inside. Clinging to the walls of

> Choose the path that is just and true.

the cave, you feel roughness beneath your hands. You see that words are carved in the walls:

"Choose the path that is just and true."

You realize that someone has journeyed along this path before you. You decide to heed the advice written in the stone and proceed cautiously. Soon you reach a hollow area that is more open and seems to emit light.

Now look around you. As the water and minerals drip into the cave, the minerals form tiny crystals. As the water evaporates, the minerals build up. In this way, fascinating rock formations and beautiful crystals grow over thousands of years. Sometimes they hang from the ceiling of the cave, forming a stalactite. Other times they build up from the cave floor and form stalagmites. These beautiful formations are what change even the darkest caves into hidden fantasy lands.

The gallery of stalagmites and stalactites and other amazing rock formations take your breath away, but do not touch! Touching an "active" formation causes growth to cease in that area because dirt or oil from human skin prevents water from reaching the growing formation. Enough touches, and the formation will "die." *Now do you see why you may have been set apart from some of the people in your life? You know… the touchy ones who just have to put their hands on your circumstances, dreams, and visions?*

At first, the thought of entering a cave sounded dreary; but now, can you see it? Some of the earth's most beautiful crystals and semi-precious stones were formed in the belly of a cave. You too will emerge as a jewel ready to be presented and used in a glorious way.

Take note that the water solution is deposited on the "same spot" over thousands of years (drip, drip, drip). You might feel picked on during God's process, but just know that *inside the cave, He is perfecting those things that concern you.* Just because you don't feel the mighty downpour of rain, which you so need, doesn't mean God has forgotten you. Remember, although the mineralized water that is dripping … dripping … seems tedious, it contains all the nutrients needed to give life to a new formation.

Maneuvering through the cave can be exhausting. It's enough to cause some to faint or even turn back. Slumped against the wall your eyes fall upon another carved message:

"Be not weary, continue. You will reap great benefits."

Caves are often a labyrinth of underground connective tunnels. It may seem you are spending endless time groping your way through the dark passages. But eventually you emerge and surprisingly find yourself completely on the other side of what seemed an impassable mountain.

The Birth Cave

The womb protects what is being formed inside from outside influences. It nurtures and provides shelter to something that is developing and growing.

Some identify caves as the womb of the earth, and therefore associate them with birth and regeneration. Caves are the earliest known sacred places for various cultures. Some known natural caves contain sacred springs believed to possess special healing properties. In your cave, take hold of your divine healing—physical, mental, spiritual, and emotional.

According to Bible scholars, the stable where Mary gave birth to Jesus, which is normally depicted as a wooden stall in most Christmas nativity scenes, was most likely a cave. Do not mourn your cave. Do not despise this time of being set apart. *It may be the very place where you birth your vision!*

My Cave Experience

One bitterly cold February night, by invitation of a campus minister, I joined two other college students on a visit to an off-campus church. We bundled up in coats, boots, and gloves and boarded the first of two buses that took us from campus to what seemed like the middle of nowhere. We danced around to keep warm, but our winter gear was no match for the sub-zero air seeping

> Do not despise this time of being set apart. It may be the very place where you birth your vision!

through our garments. With fingers and toes frozen, and noses and eyes running, we made a decision to head back to campus.

Just then, an old Chevy with a little old lady at the wheel pulled up and rolled down the window. "Oh yes, Bethlehem Temple Church. I know the pastor very well," she said. We piled in, greeted by the car's heater on full blast. Just as we began to thaw, she dropped us right at the front door of the church.

Though I was hesitant to respond to the altar call, I joined church that night. In my heart I knew I wanted what this experience offered and I also knew the sacrifice it would require. But in my hunger, I decided to heed to the strict teachings and traditions of the church. Women could wear no make up, jewelry, or pants. Members were not to dance or listen to secular music. I became a peculiar sight to my family and even lost most of my friends. No one followed me into the cave. It was a great disappointment to my family that I'd left the church I grew up in and had served in since childhood. *Here I was in the prime of my youth, cut off from everything the "real world" had to offer.* Among other things, I turned down an opportunity to model with Dorue et Enfants International Couture, and an audition with the popular group The New Birth.

This lifestyle left room for little else in my life, so I fasted and prayed constantly and immersed myself in the Word of God. It was a major test of obedience and submission.

Choose the path that is just and true.

To Know Him

Music was all I had left. Then I lost that too. Never before and never since has God given me a timeline for how long a test would last. But He had spoken "eighteen months" to me just before I lost my voice. I could talk, but when I opened my mouth to sing, nothing would come forth but a squeak. The best doctors and specialists could not determine the cause. Eighteen months later, my tonsils were removed and I went through a series of allergy injections. Finally I could sing again. A year and a half without music had totally stripped me. But I remained faithful.

The young people from this church visited concerts and revivals at other churches, especially when a powerhouse down-home West Virginia preacher by the name of T.D. Jakes would come to town. (Who knew that twenty years later *Time* magazine would name him America's best preacher?). The Bible tells us that when the Word is planted in our hearts, satan comes immediately to steal it away. But when you are surrounded by believers who are likewise in the Word, when it is all you know and all you know to do, it makes the enemy's job a little more difficult. My unadorned appearance alone set me apart from others, and during this time in my life, in this stage of my Christian development, that was a good thing. *Without external influences, I was able to receive and hold on to the Word.* The Word therefore was "preserved" in me, and remains to this day.

Today, when I hear someone preaching new doctrine, the Word rises up in me as a witness for or against it. I may not be the best of Bible scholars, but I sure know enough to discern truth and align it with the Word.

I was so hungry, I caught two, sometimes three buses several times a week to get to the house of God. One snowy day as I walked into service, the pastor stopped mid-sermon to make an announcement to the transportation ministry: "Anytime she walks through that door, you are to see her home." Thing is, I was no longer staying nearby on campus, but was back home at my parents', an hour away. On Sundays, I slept in the church between morning and evening service and worked for tips in the church dining hall just to get bus fare! *What was I after? I had to know Him!*

Bishop Thomas watched over me as my spiritual father and led me through the cave. He showed me the Word of God as I'd never seen it (beautiful stalagmites and stalactites)! Although he was a man in his seventies, he always called me "friend." People thought it was strange. I had to be prepared when I walked in to hear him say, "Friend, come sing me a song!"

Oh, how I miss him. When he died, I did not want to sing at his funeral. But I knew I had to honor him and not deny his last request of me: "Friend, come sing me a song!" I thought I'd lost that term of endearment. But in a dream the Lord said, "It was I who called you friend."

Entering this cave resulted in the most rewarding experience of my life. I emerged "full of the Word." I braved the coldness and criticism of the outside world, but was warmed by an internal eternal flame. From this life of suffering and persecution was laid a sure foundation for future spiritual growth and development.

MY TRUE CALLING

While cleaning the church one Saturday, the Lord spoke into my ear. What He spoke went directly into my spirit; my brain did not get a chance to process it. All I can tell you is that my tongue immediately proclaimed, "I can teach!" (It wasn't a question I had asked God or even considered. I had simply made myself *available* for His use.) I began to have understanding of some dreams I had since childhood, that teaching and exhorting was my true calling, expressed through many avenues: music, writing, drama, and other gifts.

This was revealed to me in the cave!

LESSONS LEARNED IN THE CAVE

1. *God is our Source.*

> *"He sealeth up the hand of every man; that all men may know His work."*
>
> (Job 37:7)

If you've ever had a time in your life when it seemed as though no one you asked for help could or would meet your need, consider this: Perhaps God wants to teach you that people are not your source. It is human nature to latch on to the person who solved your last problem—to run back to them every time you have need--until you find yourself holding cupped hands under a dry spout, pleading, begging, even getting angry because it isn't producing what you want. Friend, the water is flowing freely from another fountain.

We as humans also believe in tit-for-tat. If I gave you water from my faucet, you should give me water from yours. But although we are promised blessings for giving to others, those blessings come from God. If you show love to someone and they don't give love in return, someone else will. *Sometimes the Lord will seal the hand of man so that you will look to Him alone as your source.* Even those who once blessed you in times past are unable to, at least for a season.

> Sometimes the Lord will seal the hand of man so that you will look to Him alone as your source.

2. *Promotion comes from God*

Your employment is not your source. It is a vehicle through which God can funnel His provision. Your boss is not the final word on your elevation and increase. I found this out when a supervisor that didn't care very much for me (and told me so) said that although I was a good worker, he'd decided to give me a mediocre performance rating with not much of a salary increase. A few days later, he called me back into his office and said the executive office did not sign off on his recommendation. He was "instructed" to give me an exceptional performance rating with a commendable raise! He actually laughed at himself saying, "I thought I was the boss!"

God is your promoter. *Whatever He has promised to you will manifest through whatever, or whomever He chooses.* Leave it to Him.

> *"Wealth and honor come from you alone, for you rule over everything. Power and might are in your hand, and at your discretion people are made great and given strength."*
>
> (1Chr. 29:12, NLT)

From then on I was no longer a people-pleaser. My delight is to please the Lord. Today, my obedience to God is never tested by whom or what I must forsake. *Those early years in the cave taught me how to walk alone.*

3. Follow the Leader

Careful now. Caves can be dangerous. While caves offer protection and shelter, they can also trap and imprison. In the dark, you can become disoriented among all the caverns and channels. In certain areas, the air is not breathable by humans. Some parts of the cave have stalactites that hang so low you have to crawl under them. In your cave, prepare to humble yourself below the glorious handiwork of God.

Some people never leave their cave. That is the state of their existence until death. Elijah would have died in his cave had he not heard, recognized and obeyed the voice of the Lord.

A world famous caver died in a cave. Experts say he made three key mistakes: He went alone, he did not carry the proper sources of light, and he did not tell anyone where he was going. Jesus is your guide, Jesus is your light, and Jesus knows where you're going.

The key to your survival is humility and obedience. *God knows your way out. Stay close to Him.*

> God knows your way out. Stay close to Him.

Still, it can get quite lonely in the cave, and you will need to be reminded that the Lord promised never to leave you nor forsake you. For just when you think you've been forgotten, far into the depths of the cavern you will hear the voice of Jesus calling to you just as He did to Lazarus...

"Come forth!"

Reflections Of The Journey

- God has set you alone and apart for a purpose: *restoration by isolation*.

- Your cave experience may be God's way of keeping you from corruption or protecting you from your enemies.

- What you won't bury will someday bury you.

- Whatever is holding on to you and binding you to your past is blinding you to your future.

- In the darkness of the cave, your hearing grows keener.

- Inside the cave, He is perfecting those things that concern you.

- Do not mourn your cave. It may be the very place where you birth your vision!

- God knows your way out. Stay close to Him.

The Journey Continues . . .

Chapter 16
The Perfect Storm

My flight from Dallas to Houston was delayed, as storms were brewing all over Texas. Finally, we boarded the plane. I was in the "A" group so I was happy to be able to select the first available window seat. The plane ascended into the dark skies and up through the ominous clouds. But up above the clouds, the view was quite different—clear and calm. The Lord began to speak to me about the storms of life. I'd had many that year.

Eagles's Wings

I had decided to finish my first music CD. It was an act of obedience. Everything was going great. I had finally found a musician/producer who could take my rough-drafts and put some real meat on the bones. But one thing the Lord impressed upon me was that I had been given a "window of opportunity" on this project.

As we began working on the very first song, all hell broke loose. During that time my job was threatened, our beloved church lost its building, and my marriage ended. My car needed a new transmission. The house needed repairs. My doctor found a cyst on my liver. Funds were limited, bills were mounting. *Aieeee!*

There was a storm brewing in my heart. Should I put the CD on hold? Again?

I kept hearing the word of the Lord that was given to me at the luncheon: "God has said He's told you over and over and over and over things you should be doing. And you continue to let yourself be pushed back ..." (see Chapter 3). I decided to press on.

Whatever it took, I made the sacrifice. I sold jewelry, clothes, leather, furs, and went without heat in the house and car. It was times like this when I wished I could go home for a while to see Mom and Dad, hug them, and talk to them. But they were gone. So instead, I called upon their strength, morals and work ethics. I appreciated them for instilling those character traits in me. Yes, I would make the sacrifice. I was determined to finish something.

The apostle Peter had his own stormy experience. We tend to remember how Peter took his eyes off of Jesus and sank into the raging waters of the Sea of Galilee. But before that, Peter had a moment in his life that he would never forget. In the midst of the storm, he walked on water, people! *Do you have such a moment – when you stepped out of your flesh into the anointing of God and defied all the natural circumstances around you?* Only when Peter's carnal mind began to dominate his spirit, and he heard the winds blowing and the voices of his friends telling him to get back in the boat did he began to lose faith. Getting out of the boat in the midst of a raging storm – foolish, eh?

"The pilot has turned off the fasten seatbelt sign..."

Now 20,000 miles in the air, God reminded me of His promise to give me eagle's wings, to fly above the storms. For the first time, I truly felt I was experiencing this. I was in the storm, but my course was steady, not tossed and driven as in times before. I won't lie, there were tears, but deep inside I had an incredible joy, and my music became more prophetic.

At one point, all progress on the CD came to a halt and the musician unexpectedly left town with the last three songs unfinished. Oh no! God had said that I only had a "window of opportunity." Had I blown it? I had to repent for having allowed other things to distract me, even good things like working for the church. Then I declared, "I will not die with the music inside." In a dream, a song came:

> *March faithfully onward*
> *Leave your past behind*
> *This is not like before*
> *You're going to walk through that door*
> *So answer swiftly to the call*
> *This time you won't fall*
> *Now that you're standing on*
> *Solid ground*
> *Answer swiftly to the call.*

What "call"?
I was about to find out.

The Lifeline - Sink or Swim

I stumbled through the door from work, threw my purse on the kitchen counter, and began sorting through some junk mail. The message light on my answering machine was flashing. I pushed play.

Beep! "The Pastor is going to be out of town and would like for you to bring the word Wednesday night." Beep!

Bring the *what*? I had to rewind and play it twice more. Sure, I was on the program almost every service, but that involved singing or giving the announcements. Never to "bring the word"! I wanted to stall, hesitate, until I could think of a way out of this odd request. With all the storms going on in my life, I simply did not feel qualified to stand before God's people. But "answer swiftly to the call," had been my instructions in the song God had given.

I had learned that blessings come with obedience, and if this was a test, I sure needed to pass. Besides, this was my opportunity to get out of the boat, out of my comfort zone. I called the church office to say yes. Immediately, the promises began to manifest! The musician called. He was driving back from L.A. as fast as he could. He said he "suddenly" felt impressed to hurry back and finish my tracks!

We stayed awake for twenty-one straight hours to get it done.

Then I received a word during a special Forth of July service from a visiting minister: "The studio awaits you. The microphone awaits you. Changes await you. Elevation for the song of the Lord awaits you. Pieces and puzzles of your life are coming together."

This was significant because the studio in which I wanted to record the vocals had closed. But miraculously it re-opened, then closed for good after I finished recording. By then, I was low on funds with no means to pay for artwork, duplication, etc. That's when I received an unexpected work bonus and a refund from an unexpected source. Not only was I able to pay cash for the entire CD project, but my finances began to steadily improve. Soon, all my bills were paid off. I bought the car I had been dreaming of, and was able to bless others with the overflow (part of my daily confession).

When the CD was complete I greatly rejoiced. Not because it was everything I wanted it to be. It wasn't. But because it was an act of obedience. It was birthed out of my storm.

Perhaps best of all, that memorable Wednesday night after I "brought the word," a special note came from a young mother in our congregation:

Dear Stacey,

This is something that I've been wanting to tell you for some time now. God has truly done a marvelous work in you. I have seen many people changed by God. But you, I had the joy of watching that change take place. Now your life is such an inspiration to me, it is unbelievable. You are the most beautiful person I know. You just look different!!! Your beauty shines from the inside out and it is amazing to just watch you flow. When God finishes with me, I hope to look like you from the inside out.

God Bless You
LM

I am praying for God to bless you with the desires of your heart because you deserve it! ☺

Could she see what I was feeling? I was flying on eagle's wings!

Ingredients of A Perfect Storm

Along your journey you are sure to face many storms. Some will be divine (water-walking experiences), some man-made, and some self-made. The term "perfect storm" was originally used to indicate the three meteorological entities that must mesh in a perfect manner in order to create the storm. *A perfect storm is a situation where, by the series of specific events, what might have been a minor issue ends up being magnified to proportions that are out of control.* In such a situation, it is clear that if one element were removed from the mix, the whole matter might have been prevented. But because all the right things were in the mix, the situation balloons. This is a storm that:

- Gets your attention
- Had pre-existing circumstances to induce storm conditions
- Brings you to a point of decision
- Tests your strengths and your weaknesses
- You can't get through alone

Storms cause us to run and take cover in the safest place possible. *The purpose of your storm is to move you from one place to another, cause you to take cover, and set you back on the path of purpose!*

The circumstances that come into our lives help shape our destiny. Many people have weathered storms and lived to tell about them. What can you learn from their stories? Your job is to go through the storm and live to tell about it.

Looking back over my own situation, I had chosen logic over wisdom and made a bad decision. It was an element of my perfect storm. But I

> A perfect storm is a situation where, by the series of specific events, what might have been a minor issue ends up being magnified to proportions that are out of control.

> It is your perfect storm. You must go through it to meet your destiny on the other side.

remember Sister's reaction while previewing the photos for my CD cover and finding one where it seemed I was LOL (laughing out loud), "How could you go through all the drama you've been through this year and still have all that joy?" she asked. The fact that I could laugh, at least for the photo shoot, symbolized the CD's theme and title, *My Destiny*. So that's the photo we chose.

The storm you are in has just the right ingredients to bring out the best in you (or the worst), to identify your strengths and weaknesses. Will it be a small gust of wind or a mighty hurricane, you ask?

Whatever it takes!

It is *your* perfect storm. You must go through it to meet your destiny on the other side. You were made to survive it. So hold your head up and don't let it sink your boat.

The Land of Oz – How Did I Get Here?

Recall some of your life's storms. Did you really have calm, sunny skies one second and hurricane conditions the next?

No doubt, you had warnings. Consider the following questions and record your answers in the exercise at the end of the chapter:

- What conditions were present before this storm unleashed in your life?
- Who was in your life?
- Where did your storm originate? Track what was going on around you.
- Track what was going on within you. How were you feeling and behaving at the time?
- When was it just "bad weather" and when did it actually become a severe storm? What were the indicators?
- When was the last clear opportunity you had of avoiding severe conditions or calamity?

The Perfect Storm

Although deceptively calm, a salmon-pink sunrise and an ill-wind warns that a hurricane is brewing. A storm watch will be issued first, then a warning. They advise: "You are in the path of a storm, take shelter or prepare for the worst." But even with mandatory evacuations, some folks decide to wait it out at home. Or they plan hurricane parties in local hotels. Whatever decisions people make before the storm, they do so having been made fully aware of the consequences.

Dorothy, a famed fictional native of Kansas, was no stranger to powerful storms. She knew what the skies looked like when a storm was brewing and when to take shelter. So how was it that she was without cover when the tornado touched down? She ran away with her dog, Toto, rather than to risk losing him. And wouldn't you? He had been her constant companion, her security blanket that comforted her in her loneliness.

Toto represented the thing she could not let go of, even in the face of imminent danger and to her own detriment. It sent her on a journey to a strange land in search of a false prophet. But Dorothy learned some valuable lessons about life and herself. The Tin Man, the Scarecrow, and the Lion all represented her fears. Through her storm in Oz, she learned that love, wisdom, and courage were already inside of her. And she learned that the thing she ran away from, yet was desperately seeking, was with her all the time: home.

When I see Toto all bound up in Dorothy's arms, I think of how I must look to God when I'm holding tight and clinging to my own issues, fears, and low self-esteem.

What do you see?

When the Storm Stalls

Tropical Storm Allison stalled over Houston for many days. I had no idea how bad it was until I saw people on the news stranded in cars and buses all along I-45. They had been there all night. When the flood waters finally receded, Houston was a sight to see. Soggy carpets were piled high on front lawns. Furniture and appliances too. Cars and trucks were overturned in ditches. At the time, we had no idea we were living through the worst tropical storm in history, even earning the right to have her name retired.

I used to wonder why people bought beach homes on Galveston Island, knowing the Gulf of Mexico is prime target for hurricanes and tropical storms. Why invest in property with that much likelihood of it being washed out to sea, or to see your roof go sailing across the bay? Property owners I've spoken to have an easy going, laid back attitude about it. They simply say, "We'll rebuild."

You're likely to encounter many storms in life. Perhaps you are in one now. Certainly you may have lost much, but not all. Whatever is lost to you in your storm, you too can rebuild!

Take inventory of what remains:

- Your life
- Your mind
- A loving friend or family member
- A good church
- A working car
- A skill or education
- Your faith

> If you still have a dream, you still have a future!

If you have the strength to try again, you have somewhere to start. If you still have a dream, you still have a future!

When a storm stalls over your life:
- Hold your head up
- Don't focus on what you are going *through*, but what you are going *to*. What's on the other side of your storm?
- What is this process designed to produce in you?
- Recognize when a lifeline is being thrown to you
- Recognize who your lifeline is (Almighty God), and be obedient

Search And Rescue - A Rainbow In The Storm

The Lord may send a lifeline to encourage you to hold on and to let you know He hasn't forgotten you. Don't overlook or dismiss God's rainbows.

A dear church mother from Pennsylvania was a frequent visitor to our congregation. She was greatly beloved and highly esteemed for her wise and kind, but frank words. As I was busily organizing the ministerial staff for a grand event, she summoned me to meet with her in one of the church classrooms. I was quite nervous, having great respect for this lady. We sat facing each other as she told me that the storm I was going through was all about what was on the inside of me.

She instructed me to run hot water over a towel from the kitchenette that was along the wall in the classroom. "As hot as you can get it." I did so. "Now wring it out real good." What she did next so humbled me that I was immediately reduced to tears.

She placed my feet in her lap and began to wash them with the hot towels. She prayed and spoke healing to my body and told me not to be alarmed about a certain health issue I was experiencing, because it was all about the cleansing.

Next, she anointed my feet with oil, then paused and looked around. She asked me to bring her a bottle of perfume from across the room. While spraying the perfume on one foot, then the other she announced, "The Lord calls you His ambassador. Your footsteps will draw people in well-known circles to Christ like a sweet perfume."

A cleansing, an anointing, and a sending forth. My God. *Right there in the midst of my storm, the Lord was anointing my footsteps for the Journey.*

Let Go and Trust

When you know your destiny is in reach, you get a certain rhythm going, and the excitement is almost unbearable. But what happens when the path ends? When the next step doesn't show up like before? You know it's there. You can feel it, almost taste it, but you can't see it. You're willing, even anxious to take the next step. You put one foot out, but don't feel anything. You reach with your hand, hoping to grab onto something. Again, nothing.

Go ahead and step out. Go ahead and reach.

There will be something to grab onto. Or, in mid-air, a beautiful thing will happen.

You will fly!

You will mount up with wings and soar to your destination.

Storm of the Century

As Hurricane Katrina was making landfall, I was performing live on Daystar TV in southeast Houston. Afterward, while having lunch with the other show guests, we got word that many New Orleans residents were trapped on rooftops by rising waters. The nation was glued to the twenty-four-hour newscasts, watching the tragic events unfold. Later, busloads of weary evacuees began arriving in Houston.

Within a few days, I was assigned to cover media at the Houston Astrodome and Reliant Center. "Dome City" was now the new home for our New Orleans neighbors.

I visited with families inside the Dome, distributing bottled water and teddy bears. They were so thankful and appreciative, and said whenever New Orleans was restored, anyone showing up with a Houston ID would be treated famously there. Signs in the Dome read: The "H" in Houston stands for heart, and "Houston, the new city of angels." In my estimation, those evacuees were the amazing ones—so resilient, so patient. The Big Easy.

"I'm a prayer warrior!" one lady announced as she stood in the door of our tent in the Dome parking lot. Everyone looked puzzled. I stepped forward and greeted her, hugged her, and basically just let her talk. She told me terrifying stories of events occurring in both the Houston and New Orleans shelters—rapes of women and children. She attributed her survival to her faith and her commission to pray for her fallen city. After that, I couldn't sleep. I cried everyday of that assignment. In my journal I simply wrote, "My heart hurts."

⁖ The Perfect Storm ⁖

Speak to Your Storm

I checked the messages on my home voice recorder one final time before evacuating Houston for Hurricane Rita. A message from Kenneth Copeland Ministries let us know that we were being covered in prayer, but also urged us not to sit and watch the storm move closer, but to go outside, walk around our houses and speak into the atmosphere, commanding Rita to dissipate and do no harm. I complied. Though Houston was dead on target for Rita to make landfall, she made a curve to the northeast and Houston was spared.

> By the authority of Jesus Christ you can speak to your storm.

By the authority of Jesus Christ you can speak to your storm. Jesus permitted the storm in Peter's life as an opportunity to demonstrate faith. But as our example, Jesus also spoke to stormy situations, saying, "Peace be still." And the storm ceased (Mark 4:39).

Give permission and submit to what God wants the storm to accomplish in you. You can set the boundaries.

Say to your storm:

> *You may have your perfect work in me,*
> *But you may not overtake or destroy me.*
> *I will go through, I will not go under.*
> *My victory is sure, my destiny is secure.*

You know you have passed the test when you can still say at the end of your storm, "Nothing shall separate me from the love of God."

On the first of December I awoke and recalled a dream I had the night before. Oddly, it was not visual. No people, no scenery, no colors. Just two words lingering in the atmosphere:

> *Unstuck*
> *Unscathed*

I knew the Lord had spoken them. They were resting upon me like the morning dew.

I was going to be alright. The year was ending and so was my storm.

Will the Sun Rise Again?

While reading this chapter, you have probably recalled some personal "hurricane" moments. Or perhaps you are having such a moment today. Just because the sun isn't shining doesn't mean that God's not with you. Storm season can be an unlovely time. Surroundings are dark, damp, and dreary. You often ask "Why?" Or "Why me?" You may be wounded; you may feel low. But remember, *you are dearly loved!* Your storm is about the wonderful things God wants to do in you and through you.

> Your storm will end. Even giants sleep.

If you know someone who is going through a storm, show them love, until the storm passes over. Friend, you will weather this storm, and the sun will rise again. When have you ever known the sun not to rise?

Your storm will end. Even giants sleep.

Reflections Of The Journey

- The purpose of your storm is to cause you to take cover, move you from one place to another, and set you back on the path of purpose.

- The storm you are in has just the right ingredients to bring out the best in you.

- Whatever is lost to you in your storm, you can rebuild.

- Your job is to go through the storm and live to tell about it.

- In your storm, don't overlook or dismiss God's rainbows.

- It is your perfect storm. You must go through it to meet your destiny on the other side.

- By the authority of Jesus Christ you can speak to your storm and set boundaries.

- Go ahead and step out. Go ahead and reach. There will be something to grab onto, or there in mid-air a beautiful thing will happen. You will fly!

The Journey Continues . . .

Exercise

OZ - How Did I Get Here?

Think about life's storms. Now did you really have sunny skies one second and hurricane conditions the next? No doubt, you had warnings. Think about:

What conditions were present in your life *before* this storm unleashed?

Who was in your life?

Who caused you to be complacent?

Who warned you?

Where did your storm originate? Track what was going on around you:

Track what was going on *within* you:

What was the last clear chance you had of avoiding severe conditions or calamity?

What would you do differently to avoid this storm?

Exercise
Perfect Storm Inventory
(What Remains?)

You're likely to encounter many storms in life. Perhaps you are in one now.
Certainly you may have lost much, but not all.
Whatever is lost to you in your storm, you can rebuild!

Take inventory of what remains:

- ❏ Your life
- ❏ Your mind
- ❏ A loving friend or family member
- ❏ A good church

- ❏ A working car
- ❏ A skill or education
- ❏ Your faith

OTHER:

- ❏ _____
- ❏ _____
- ❏ _____
- ❏ _____

If you have the strength to try again, you have somewhere to start.

If you still have a *dream*, you still have a *future!*

Chapter 17
Water in the Desert

Everyone goes through a dry season — a time when nothing in your life is growing, being fruitful or productive. You hunger for something good to happen. You thirst. It seems every opportunity for breakthrough turns out to be a mirage.

Are there parched areas of your life? Maybe a business has dried up, or the opportunity to pursue a career, education, or ministry has fallen through. In spite of burning sand, blistered feet and eyes blinded by dust storms, you will have to trust.

In the desert, you have been called to a dry place so that you will thirst for Him.

> In the desert, you have been called to a dry place so that you will thirst for Him.

Sedona

It was my birthday, and I had journeyed to Arizona to help a friend through a rough time. But thinking of me, she called a mutual friend. "She has to see Sedona," they conspired.

On a beautiful Sunday morning, the Chevy Suburban carried us up a narrow, steep and windy road. As we climbed higher and higher, the mysterious rocks seemed to whisper, "Come learn of my lifelong secrets." Sedona has small town charm, quaint shops of baskets, pottery, and jewelry, and ancient villages. But most of all Sedona has a soul.

Breathtaking views of the majestic red rock formations were silhouetted against the winter sky. Nestled in a hollow between two mounds of rust-colored mountains was the Chapel of the Holy Cross, a refuge from the storms of life in this thirsty landscape. At the top of the hill a sign posted by the door of the chapel greeted us: "Peace To All Who Enter."

The chapel was a symbol of hope crying out "Rest, restore, rejuvenate your body, mind, and spirit!" It was unexpectedly refreshing.

Passing of the Peace

Back at the office in Houston, I returned just in time for our favorite corporate volunteer function, Habitat for Humanity. We were building homes for Oprah's Angel network to house several Hurricane Katrina families.

Hammers rang throughout the neighborhood as Angel Lane bustled with volunteer crews climbing ladders, hammering plywood, and shingling rooftops. Our pleasant and grateful new homeowners worked along side of us the entire day; then we shared a traditional New Orleans King Cake. Toward the end of the work day, I invited the work crew to sign the framed walls before they were sheet-rocked.

Above the front door I wrote, "Peace to all who enter," duplicating the Sedona chapel's greeting.

I Thirst

In your desert, you'd give anything to quench your soul. Exhausted and dehydrated, you feel your body surrendering to a state of desolation. Unable to go one more step, you flop to the earth and let the soft, shifting sand have its way. Although your eyes are heavy, off in the distance you make out what appears to be a dingy, abandoned tent. A refuge.

Water in the Desert

Mustering your last ounce of strength, you crawl to reach it. After all, night is falling and you are grateful for a place to rest for a while, or maybe for a lifetime.

> You were anointed for more.

Cautiously, you part the opening of the dark tent, but something dangling atop the opening strikes your forehead. Seems like a picture frame or a sign. You duck around it and continue to feel your way inside, over to a tattered mat. Drifting off to sleep you can't resist thoughts of hopelessness and despair.

Rest doesn't come easy in these dry and dreary surroundings. But morning comes quickly, and somehow the dingy tent seems brighter and more colorful. And oh yeah, there's that sign that almost conked you in the head at the opening of the tent. You rise to read it and are overcome by its words: *"You were anointed for more."*

Simple. But you know instinctively it's speaking to you and telling you that *you cannot remain in this state of unfruitfulness. It is time to leave your desert.* But not until you understand why you are there.

Three Reasons For Being Trapped in the Desert:

1. Unforgiveness

Harboring ill feelings against others causes you to dry up inside.

> *"... a broken spirit drieth the bones."*
> (Prov. 17:22)

> Harboring ill feelings against others causes you to dry up inside.

2. Rebellion

Hearing the Word but not obeying. Unpaid vows or unfinished business. Ignoring instruction from God. Intent on handling things your way.

> *"... the rebellious dwell in a dry land."*
> (Ps. 68:6)

Refusing to walk in your purpose or pursue your destiny.

> "... how long are ye slack to go in to possess the land which the Lord God of your fathers hath given you?"
>
> (Josh. 18:3)

3. No worship – no rain!

You've lost your passion for the Lord, or have become lazy in seeking Him.

Are you ready for things to start growing again in your life? Then take in what I'm about to tell you and move on it without hesitation. Repent of any disobedience, wrong decisions, or lack of follow-through on matters you have left unattended. Forgive and release any hurt or wrong that was done to you. Then lift your hands and worship like you never have – Worship brings rain!

Worship brings rain!

> "O God, thou art my God; early will I seek thee: my soul thirsteth for thee, my flesh longeth for thee in a dry and thirsty land, where no water is; To see thy power and thy glory, so as I have seen thee in the sanctuary ... my lips shall praise thee ... I will lift up my hands in thy name. My soul shall be satisfied ... and my mouth shall praise thee with joyful lips."
>
> (Ps. 63:1-5)

Drink of the water He gives, it is necessary to your survival. Drink of waters of healing, forgiveness, and obedience. Because *until you drink of them, your desert season will not end.*

The Waters Shall Flow

> "And it shall come to pass in that day, that the mountains shall drop down new wine, and the hills shall flow with milk, and all the rivers of Judah shall flow with waters, and a fountain shall come forth of the house of the Lord,"
>
> (Joel 3:18)

Healing Streams

Streams may be small, but they serve a great purpose. They can get into places that rivers can't. You know, *those hard to reach places like the pain you hide in your heart?* Streams are tiny tributaries that cleanse and carry nutrients. They flow into cracked dry places and soften bitterness and anger.

> Drink of the water He gives, it is necessary to your survival.

God's grace is a stream of living water in the desert. No place is too small for Him to reach. Nothing is too insignificant to touch God's heart. *You matter.*

Beaumont, Texas, had become a dry town after Hurricane Rita. No stores, restaurants or gas stations were operating. I emerged from the company RV with bottled water for a couple that had entered our tent to have their claim settled. In the squelching heat, the wife's hair and make-up were amazingly perfect. Yet something was going on inside that wasn't picture perfect. Slowly she began to tell me her troubles. As I returned to the RV to gather some information for her, I heard the door open behind me. She literally fell into my arms, sobbing. I helped her to the sofa and let her just tell me what was hurting so bad. She had been betrayed by some people she had helped back in Louisiana who had now turned their backs on her during this time of need.

I comforted her and advised her not to look for her reward in people. I told her that beyond the pain she needed to realize that "What you make happen for others, God will make happen for you". I got her focused on what she had remaining on the inside and how she was to continue making a difference. That spoke to her. The more we talked about destiny and purpose, the more alive she became. She went running out to her husband with renewed faith in their future.

I was her healing stream. You can also be a stream. Find some small way to serve Him. And touch someone's life who thinks they are forgotten and out of reach of God's love.

Having worked two unprecedented back-to-back major hurricanes, I was quite weary. I missed my friends and family and sipping tea in my favorite green chair by the fireplace. I missed church. I missed having fresh, plentiful water flowing from my faucets. Sharing a spooky hotel with scruffy guys was getting quite old.

Nevertheless, my job required that I stay there to be accessible as the media spokesperson (or as my coworkers teasingly called me, the TV spokes model). It felt like everything in my life was on hold until I completed this assignment.

Toward the end of my time there, a restaurant finally reopened on I-10. And was I glad!

As I was seated, a lady and a small boy were preparing to leave.

"Are you from this area?" she asked.

"No ma'am, I'm from Houston."

"Well, we just want to thank you for coming in and helping us."

As I was about to respond, she leaned in closer and whispered, "It's time for you to take your pictures."

"Ma'am?"

"It is time for you to take your pictures."

However unexpected, I recognized the word from the Lord. As I stood up, a fresh fire rushed through me from the top of my head, down through my legs. I hugged her. She repeated slowly:

"It...is...time, honey. It... is... time."

I knew what pictures she was talking about. I had been putting it off, you know, until I was thinner and prettier. But just to know God was thinking of me out in the middle of nowhere energized me enough to complete my assignment.

He will bring you water in the desert.

Mighty Rivers

Are you a river or a reservoir?

Streams are tiny tributaries, but rivers are like veins and arteries carrying life-blood throughout the land. Rivers transport items that are essential to our everyday lives. As a river, you can be used to enhance lives because God can use you to get what He needs from one place to another, from one person to another. *If He can place resources in your hands and trust that you will carry out His assignment and be a blessing to others, you are a river!*

When God wants to open the floodgates of heaven, that's the time for you to move in purpose. Stop waiting for the perfect moment to release your gifts and talents to bless others. What are you waiting for? What are you storing up for the future?

> Your gifts and abilities are not intended to stay stored up inside of you

You are a river, not a reservoir. *Your gifts and abilities are not intended to stay stored up inside of you,* but shared among others.

You are a mighty river.

Let it flow!

Sea of Forgetfulness - A place where you release your fears

All rivers flow to meet the seas. They all long to know what's out there. What else is there for me? What secrets, mysteries, and treasures? The seas are mightier than we know.

> *"And what He did unto the army of Egypt, unto their horses, and their chariots; how He made the waters of the Red Sea to overflow them as they pursued after you, and how the LORD hath destroyed them unto this day."*
>
> (Deut. 11:4)

The army of Egypt was Israel's enemy, and it was in hot pursuit as Israel left the land where they had been slaves for over 400 years. Your enemies also pursue you with the intent to oppress you, steal your health, your family, your peace, your opportunities, your very breath. Do not fear. *God has a Red Sea for every enemy in your life!*

Know that the sea that seems to stand between you and your blessing may serve a divine purpose, as I learned while still working in Beaumont. One evening, I booked myself on a cruise.

Yes, that was a vacation I figured I wouldn't cancel as I had all the others that year. Months later aboard the ship, I was glad I'd made the reservation. While getting dressed for dinner, the Lord impressed upon me to write down the things I counted as unachieved goals, unfulfilled dreams, disappointments, and failures in my life. I thought that was odd, because I wasn't feeling down about anything. But I made the list as things came to my remembrance, and left it on the coffee table.

When I returned later that evening, I had forgotten about the list. I picked it up, and it was as if the breeze from the balcony was beckoning me. I stepped out into the night air, the silvery stars glistening against the midnight sky. In a fierce gust of wind, the thin paper was about to get away from me. As I was desperately trying to hold on to it, God said, "Let it go."

It was like time stood still. At first I looked around, not wanting to get in trouble for littering. Then I remembered obedience is better than sacrifice. *"Let it go,"* He impressed upon me. *"Throw it into the sea of forgetfulness."* Big tears filled my eyes. I had no idea what God was up to.

I stood before the sea that was so much bigger than I. In that moment, I released my past into the depths. At first, a gust of the wind snatched it from me. Then it began to flutter downward, softly and slowly, as if gliding on an angel's wing, until it was no more.

The sea is a place where you forget about your past and where you understand the true meaning of forgiveness. When the future God places before you is so much greater than your past, you have no desire to remember! *Whatever it is that you will not release is what is holding you captive.*

> When the future God places before you is so much greater than your past, you have no desire to remember!

Treasures of the Seas

It was then that I understood I wasn't just enjoying a much needed vacation. *God had called me out into the deep.* But what He spoke next totally astonished me:

"Command the sea to yield its treasures and abundance."

What? I couldn't believe my ears. Not because it sounded so strange, but because it sounded familiar. Was it a Scripture? It had to be. I couldn't have made that up!

And so I commanded the waters to bring forth abundance and give up her hidden treasures to me, and all secrets, mysteries and treasures that had been hidden in my life to be revealed. I spent the rest of the evening searching for that Scripture. I didn't find it until I got back home.

Once I found the Scripture at home, it *was* settled. God had spoken.

> *"They shall call the people unto the mountain; there they shall offer sacrifices of righteousness: for they shall suck of the abundance of the seas, and of treasures hid in the sand."*
>
> (Deut. 33:19)

He said the ability to draw people to the mountain of the Lord speaks of influence. And that the priceless treasure, once hidden away where none could find, would soon be revealed.

> *"Then you will look and be radiant, and your heart will throb and swell with joy; the wealth on the seas will be brought to you, to you the riches of the nations will come."*
>
> (Isa. 60:5, NIV)

Oceans of Opportunity

When you stand before the ocean, you can't help but be in complete awe and respect it. You realize how small you are and how great God really is. Who can know the extent of His greatness?

Oceans connect our worlds, nation to nation. The ocean is no respecter of persons. It has washed the feet both of kings and slaves on its shores.

The ocean is a place of creativity and fertility. It represents your greatest growth potential and ability to reach out and reproduce the virtue that is within you. As it is endless and boundless, so is your opportunity to speak to nations!

Like old buried ship wrecks, the dreams, prayers, and frustrations of multitudes have sunk into the depths of the waters. But some reemerge and wash up along the coastline, right at your feet. You respond by launching out into the deep and allowing the supernatural power of

> Hush now, Divinity is speaking.

God to flow through you and stretch you beyond human capabilities, from nation to nation.

Friend, an ocean of anointing is upon you! You shall carry good tidings to the poor, heal the broken hearted and set free those that are captive.

Possibly, my most favorite thing to do in the whole world is to walk along a quiet beach. Something about the water makes me feel closer to God. The ocean waves seem to say, *"Hush now, Divinity is speaking."*

I love to feel the warm, foamy waves on my feet. I always think of the ebb and flow of the tide as blessings coming in to greet me and blessings I send out. Wave upon wave.

> *"And all these blessings shall come upon thee, and overtake thee, if you will hearken to the voice of the Lord thy God."*
>
> (Deut. 28:2)

Caring streams become rivers. Faithful rivers become oceans with the greatest potential to change the world.

Come To The Waters

> *"Ho, everyone that thirsteth, come ye to the waters, and he that hath no money; come ye, and eat; yea, come, buy wine and milk without money and without price."*
>
> (Isa. 55:1)

God will lead you to healing streams and bring you to rivers that flow. You will stand beside the sea and make your declarations, and you will usher in new victories with the waves of the oceans. Your desert can be quenched with the water He gives.

> *"...if any man thirst, let him come unto Me and drink. He that believeth on Me, as the Scripture hath said, out of his belly shall flow rivers of living water."*
>
> (John 7:37-38)

Something else to consider in your dry season: "There is no growth without management." In other words:

> "God will not allow things to grow in your life until you are ready and positioned to manage them."
>
> -- Dr. Myles Munroe

Are there instructions or responsibilities God gave you that you did not carry out, or began but did not nurture? As you demonstrate your faithfulness in these areas, you should begin to see your vision coming back to life.

Certain things only grow in dry places, such as blooming cactus, desert lilies, and summer poppy. How is it possible for beautiful things to grow in dry places?

> "...Her desert will blossom like Eden, her barren wilderness like the garden of the LORD. Joy and gladness will be found there. Songs of thanksgiving will fill the air."
>
> (Isa. 51:3, NLT)

In the desert, you must speak life to everything around you, and position yourself for management and growth. And you must remember that worship brings rain.

Dry and parched on the outside, yet inside you are immersed in faith and assurance. That is your moment, when you know you are ready to emerge from your dry season and walk into your promised land!

> In the desert, you must speak life to everything around you.

Reflections Of The Journey

- You have been called to a dry place so that you will thirst for Him.

- Three reasons for being trapped in the desert: unforgiveness, rebellion, and lack of worship. Worship brings rain!

- Drink of the water He gives, because until you drink of it, your desert season will not end.

- You are a mighty river, not a reservoir. Let it flow!

- God has a Red Sea for every enemy in your life.

- When the future God places before you is so much greater than your past, you have no desire to remember!

- In the desert you must speak life to everything around you.

"Hush now, Divinity is speaking." Wave upon wave, an ocean of anointing is upon you!

The Journey Continues . . .

Exercise

Trapped in the Desert

What will you begin doing immediately to end your dry season?

Address all that apply:

Unforgiveness

Rebellion

Lack of Worship

Part IV
Inherit the Earth

"Our deepest fear is not that we are inadequate. Our deepest fear is that we are powerful beyond measure. It is our light, not our darkness, that frightens us most....Your playing small does not serve the world. There is nothing enlightened about shrinking so that people won't feel insecure around you. We were born to make manifest the glory of God that is within us. It's not just in some of us; it's in all of us."

–as quoted by Nelson Mandela

Chapter 18
Journey to the Palace

The journey has been long and treacherous. But you've learned to navigate the geography in your life, and in doing so, to take dominion of your world. If only you'd known where you were headed you'd have been more focused, motivated, and determined. Am I right? At the beginning of the journey, you were not quite ready for your promise, but now you have learned a very important thing: The purpose of the journey is not to arrive. The purpose of the journey is to "become."

And now, you are able to receive this next revelation: *He has prepared "a place" for you!*

Let's explore that special place, shall we?

Destiny Revealed

Did your childhood dreams include visions of living in a castle, palace, or overseeing a wealthy kingdom?

By definition a palace is a royal residence, a seat of government or religion. This isn't just some place you stumble upon while house hunting. You are there either by inheritance or through reward of battle.

The palace we are journeying to is not a literal place, not a physical place, yet not a fantasy island. It is a:
- Place of influence
- Place of divine order
- Place of divine provision and protection

It is the place your journey has been leading you to!

The palace is your place of divine destiny, where your gifts and talents are being used to do what you were sent by God to do on Earth, flowing in purpose, and influencing matters that are important to His Kingdom! It is a place where God not only blesses you, but makes you to be a blessing.

Picture it: You are the king, and all is well. Tell us about your kingdom.

My kingdom?

Yes, everybody has one. Whatever God has given you dominion over or assigned you to oversee is your kingdom. You may be called to government, business, media, family ministry, etc. The Kingdom is everywhere! Tell us, who is in your kingdom? What are the issues, goals, and challenges? What are your assets?

Finish the sentence, "My kingdom is rich in _____."
What are your successes, your gifts, your strengths?

> Whatever God has given you dominion over or assigned you to oversee is your kingdom.

What is your history? What have you conquered or overcome? Every kingdom has enemies that threaten its existence. Do you know who your adversaries are? Do you recognize their tactics? What comes against you every time you try to excel in some area? Perhaps not the enemies of Israel, the Hittites or the Amorites. But how about the "Debt-ites" or the "Alcohol-ites"? You can testify of the battles you have won in that area and the victories you have been rewarded. Share how your good God delivered you!

Who are your heroes? Who has counseled you, mentored you, and prayed you through?

Complete the "My Kingdom Assessment" exercise at the end of the chapter.

Who is on Your Throne?

Picture the house of your dreams. Now suppose for a moment that you received a certified letter on the official letterhead of your city government, notifying you that according to city property records, you are the owner of a grand estate in the most upscale area of your town. After research, you verify this is no joke; it's legit. However, you also learn that someone else has been occupying this property for generations, and you will have to battle in court to obtain legal documents which allow you to evict this tenant and legally take back your land. The current resident has been living like a king on this palatial estate. Who is this king sitting on your throne? Would you fight for it?

> *"Rise ye up, take your journey, and pass over the river Arnon: behold, I have given into thine hand Sihon the Amorite, king of Heshbon, and his land: begin to possess it, and contend with him in battle."*
>
> (Deut. 2:24)

> If you want to inherit the kingdom, warfare is not optional!

If you want to inherit the kingdom, warfare is not optional!

What is in Your Throne?

Whatever is sitting on your throne, aside from the things of God, is keeping you from seeing the glory of the Lord manifested in your life. It may be a person you idolize or have allowed to manipulate you. It may be money, sex, pride, drugs, or any other thing that has rule over you. It could be a career or anything you have exalted to the point that it influences or controls everything you do. Until that thing dies or is dethroned, you will never be able to see the fullness of the vision God has for you. *Let this be the year that you vow to have no other gods before Him, and let the glory of the Lord fill the temple!*

Earthly Kings

In an episode of the vintage TV show *The Honeymooners,* Ralph demands that his wife, Alice, do what he tells her. When she questions it, he says "Because I'm the king!" To which she replies, "The king of *what?*" Her face is distorted; her voice drenched in sarcasm. Poor Ralph.

Jesus Christ was sent to earth and proclaimed to be King of kings and Lord of lords. *He is King over all earthly kings.* So who are the earthly kings? Consider this statement:

> *"God has called you to be a king in this time to rule and to exercise influence for the Kingdom of God."*
>
> -- Rev. Bernice King
> (at the funeral of Coretta Scott King)

Was she right? Consider these Scriptures:

> *"And God said, Let us make man in our image, after our likeness: and let them have dominion over the fish of the sea, and over the fowl of the air, and over the cattle, and over all the earth, and over every creeping thing that creepeth upon the earth."*
>
> (Gen. 1:26)

> *"And God blessed them, and God said unto them, Be fruitful, and multiply, and replenish the earth, and subdue it: and have dominion over the fish of the sea, and over the fowl of the air, and over every living thing that moveth upon the earth."*
>
> (Gen. 1:28)

> *"Thou madest him to have dominion over the works of thy hands; thou hast put all things under his feet"*
>
> (Ps. 8:6)

> *"And the kingdom and dominion, and the greatness of the kingdom under the whole heaven, shall be given to the people of the saints of the most High, whose kingdom is an everlasting kingdom, and all dominions shall serve and obey him."*
>
> (Dan. 7:27)

> *"But you are a chosen generation, a royal priesthood, an holy nation, a peculiar people; that you should show forth the praises of Him who hath called you out of darkness into His marvelous light."*
>
> (1 Pet. 2:9)

> *"And hath made us kings and priests unto God and His father; to Him be glory and dominion forever and ever. Amen."*
>
> (Rev. 1:6)

> *"And hast made us unto our God kings and priests: and we shall reign on the earth."*
>
> Rev. (5:10)

There it is! Perhaps our childhood dreams about palaces and kingdoms weren't just fantasy. From Genesis to Revelation, God speaks to us of His desire, His vision, of our taking our places as kings and priests in the Kingdom of God. Allow me to tell it to you as God told it to me: He is not impressed with your humility when He's trying to exalt you to places of authority and influence.

Let's be clear. *God is over all kingdoms, but we carry His Kingdom within us, and we are called to reproduce it through our assignment in the earth.*

> *"... for it is the Father's good pleasure to give you the kingdom."*
>
> (Luke 12:32)

Yes, you do have a kingdom!

> For it is the Father's good pleasure to give you the kingdom.

Next time you are conversing with someone about his or her dreams and visions, you are actually visiting one another's kingdom! When you speak of aiding each other in some area, you have become allies. What your kingdom may be rich in, mine may be deficient. The sharing of resources are divine connections; we need one another. When you need access to the king, you need to know who has the king's ear. It may once have been the cupbearer, but today in today's world, it may be the administrative assistant. As allies, you could testify of the battles, strategies, and victories you have won. We can help each other defeat a common enemy.

Let us not be so careless and casual when we come together as brothers and sisters. *You are in the company of kings and queens.* Govern yourself accordingly.

Royals Heirs

Historically, a king inherits his position through the royal bloodline. Sometimes, when there was no heir and a king died, it led to bloody wars and struggles to see who would be king. God the Father sent His son Jesus to shed royal blood that you and I might become joint-heirs of the Kingdom of God.

> *"And if children, then heirs; heirs of God, and joint-heirs with Christ; if so be that we suffer with him, that we may be also glorified together."*
>
> (Rom 8:17)

> *"And now that you belong to Christ, you are the true children of Abraham. You are his heirs, and God's promise to Abraham belongs to you."*
>
> (Gal. 3:29, NLT)

As royal heirs, the promises of Abraham belong to us! All those who belong to Christ as born-again believers are heirs to the promise. What is the promise?

> *"I will make you into a great nation, and I will bless you; I will make your name great, and you will be a blessing. I will bless those who bless you, and whoever curses you I will curse; and all peoples on earth will be blessed through you."*
> (Gen. 12:2, 3 NIV)

Through *you* shall all the families of the earth be blessed!

> *"Now the Lord had said unto Abram, Get thee out of thy country, and from thy kindred, and from thy father's house, unto a land that I will show thee."*
> (Gen. 12: 1)

> We all have a Canaan land; a place of promise, provision, dominion, and authority that the Lord has reserved for us in our lifetime.

We all have a Canaan land; a place of promise, provision, dominion, and authority that the Lord has reserved for us in our lifetime. A kingdom. In this place of influence you will be in position to touch somebody's life with God's goodness and love. *Our calling is to be fruitful and multiply, to bring increase to the Kingdom of God*, to populate the Kingdom by being instrumental in transferring not only souls, but gifts, wealth, power. *To inherit the earth!*

Are you there yet?

Work It!

God placed man in the garden to work the land, to take care of His "stuff" on earth.

> *"Thou madest him to have dominion over the works of thy hands; thou hast put all things under his feet."*
> (Ps. 8:6)

The purpose of you having a kingdom is not to exalt yourself, or fulfill your own lusts or human will. The purpose of your kingdom is that you

> The purpose of your kingdom is that you will be a demonstration of God's will being done "on earth as it is in heaven".

will be a demonstration of God's will being done *"on earth as it is in heaven"*. (Matt. 6:10).

A good king is a good steward, accountable for God's goods and how they are put to use. As overseer of the land, its people and resources, a king must work the land so that it produces a fruitful harvest. He is responsible for the well-being of his kingdom and its inhabitants (those he is assigned to serve). The king must live a life of peace, order, and prosperity so that he can effectively carry out the divine will of God.

Step Into the Palace

Now that you're becoming familiar with the idea of a kingdom, would you like to take a glimpse into your royal palace? (Only a brief tour is possible, because your true palace as designed by God can only be fully revealed to you by Him).

Some palaces are impressive, opulent structures; others are unkempt ruins. *You get to decide how well decorated your palace will be* — not with material things, but:

- Walls decked with wisdom
- Air perfumed with peace
- Halls echoing with joy
- Entry glistening with grace
- Foundation firm with truth
- Chandeliers glowing with His glorious light
- Pillars fortified with prayer
- Gardens flourishing with love
- Waterfalls flowing with worship
- Grand staircase lifting toward heaven

How spectacular!
Well, what condition will your palace be in? It's up to you.

Your Royal Court

A king is very particular about with whom he shares close quarters. Only those who are loyal to the vision and well-being of the kingdom are granted access. *Surround yourself with believers and achievers, those who will help you sustain an atmosphere of what is positive and what is possible.*

In times past, a king ruled through the order of other nobles who officiated over smaller portions of the kingdom. Who is managing your warfare (praying for you), generating finances, developing new ideas, keeping watch for open doors and opportunities? Who is on the wall watching for the hidden enemy seeking to devour your plans? Who is royal advisor? *Perhaps it is time to reassess and re-establish who qualifies to share your time and intimacy.*

Be mindful of whom you entertain in your presence. Be careful with whom you share your heart of hearts. Not everyone is happy about your beloved kingdom. Be choosey about your friends and associates. Ask the Lord to connect you with the right circle of close friends.

> *"Be careful for nothing; but in everything by prayer and supplication with thanksgiving let your request be made known unto God."*
>
> (Phil. 4:6)

Jesus had twelve disciples and a multitude of followers. But take note of who was present during the most sacred, revelatory experience He shared on earth: "Jesus took Peter, James, and John and led them up a mountain apart by themselves: and was transfigured before them" (Mark 9:2).

Why did Jesus bring only Peter, James, and John up this mountain with him? It seems they were on a different level of intimacy than the rest. Jesus trusted that they would keep this moment sacred and store it in their hearts as He requested.

In the palace there are common areas, and then there are places that are off limits to the general public. *Reserve the sacred quarters of your life as that intimate and private space in which to conduct royal business.*

Who is in *your* palace?

Life in the Palace

You've journeyed far and long to reach your promised land, the palace. Now that you are set to arrive, how will life be different? Won't there still be challenges?

Yes, adversity will still arise, but *in the palace you know who you are!* You walk in authority, having gained the wisdom and knowledge to:

> In the palace you know who you are!

- Command the mountains in your life to move.
- Walk through your valley with gracefulness and gratefulness.
- Consult the Holy Spirit for wisdom and strategy on kingdom business.
- Speak to storms, set their boundaries, and command peace.
- Release mistakes, worries, and fear into the sea of forgetfulness.
- Trust God in your loneliness to bring about restoration by isolation.
- Retreat to your secret chambers or private gardens for a divine encounter with the Master.
- Worship to bring rain into your dry places.

The World Is Waiting For You

There is a presence that exists on earth today that has never existed before–that presence is you! The mission God created you for was preordained for this specific moment in time. You are uniquely designed and engineered to fulfill it. Don't settle for the ordinary, or what's been done before. Enlarge your vision.

> "... Oh, that you would bless me and enlarge my territory! Let your hand be with me, and keep me from harm so that I will be free from pain..."
>
> (1 Chron. 4:10, NIV)

How big can you dream? That's the first question. The second is: How bad do you want it? What are you willing to commit to? Because *what you are willing to sacrifice, risk, or be responsible for determines the length and breadth of your kingdom.* Being faithful over a few things qualifies you to be ruler over many. How vast is your kingdom?

When Bill Gates first dreamed of a computer on every desk in every home, people thought it was absurd. Not only is he now laughing all the way to the bank, but has created opportunities for individuals, businesses, and ministries to connect all over the world with a simple click. *As long as you're dreaming – Dream BIG!* Envision a dream that will challenge you.

If there were absolutely, positively no constraints (time, money, people), nothing and no one to hold you back, what would you be doing? If ever there was a time to do something worthy of the cause, the time is now.

> Let the kingdom within you come forth so that lives you have been assigned to touch not wait another moment to prosper.

You haven't realized it, but *something within you was destined to be life-changing for someone else*; perhaps even world-changing. Let the kingdom within you come forth so that lives you have been assigned to touch not wait another moment to prosper.

> "For the creation waits in eager expectation for the children of God to be revealed."
>
> (Rom. 8:19, NIV)

It's time to release the dream. *The world is waiting for you!*

Rise to Royalty

Let us journey far back in time into the lives of three of examples of biblical royalty and discover their royal secrets.

Joseph

Joseph's story is about the life of a dreamer. He had the God-given ability to interpret dreams. He was

> It's time to release the dream. The world is waiting for you!

favored by his father Jacob, creating jealousy among his brothers who threw him into a pit and sold him into slavery. He was brought to Egypt where he was falsely accused and bound in prison. But even in prison his gifts continued to flow. It was his ability to interpret Pharaoh's dream that allowed him to be freed from prison and placed in the palace in authority over all the land.

Meanwhile, his father, Jacob, and all of Israel were suffering a great famine. But Joseph was in a position of influence, enabling him to bring his people from poverty to the palace.

Just one man's sacrifice worked for the good of many. His sacrifices yielded great rewards, giving rise to royalty.

Joseph experienced a difficult journey, but *he made it to the palace because he didn't allow the pit or the prison to steal his dreams.* Joseph had a revelation that he was *sent* ahead of others to do God's work. Listen to what he tells his brothers:

> *"But God sent me ahead of you ... to save your lives by a great deliverance. So then, it was not you who sent me here, but God."*
>
> (Gen. 45: 7, 8, NIV)

"But as for you, ye thought evil against me; But God meant it unto good, to bring to pass, as it is this day, to save much people alive."

(Gen. 50:20)

Like Joseph, each of us are "sent" (John 20:21). God has a unique plan for your life. The pit, the prison, and the palace may all be a part of your journey too. But everything that happens to you was foreseen by God, and if you submit your life's purpose to Him, even your mistakes become stepping stones.

"And we know that for those who love God all things work together for good, for those who are called according to his purpose."

(Rom. 8:28)

Joseph's "Royal Secrets":

- In every circumstance, Joseph remained true to who he was.
- He refused to compromise his faith in God.
- He used his gift to prosper others. It cost him dearly, but the greater sacrifice the greater the reward.

David

David began his journey as the least likely to succeed. He was the youngest, the smallest, and the most insignificant among his brethren. But inside was a mysterious dual nature in which the warrior co-existed with the poet, and the mighty king with the heart of humility.

As a shepherd boy, David learned to fight in order to defend the flocks from wild animals. In the name of the Lord he killed the giant, Goliath, just as he had slain the lion and the bear. It was his first public display of courage. He was beginning his rise to royalty.

However, the jealous king Saul sought to kill David. But David refused to lift his sword and remained a fugitive until Saul was killed in battle. When David was anointed king, He united the people of Israel and established his empire, with Jerusalem as its epicenter. He then brought the Holy Ark, which had been passed from city to city, to Jerusalem. He also laid plans to build a temple to God, which would later be carried out by Solomon, his son.

David was a true worshipper and a dedicated man who served God forty years as king. But the anointing of this king took place back when he was still a shepherd boy, long before the public coronation. At times, David's rise to greatness was intermingled with personal strife, sin, and corruption. However, despite his human faults, David poured out his repentance to God. In turn, he was greatly beloved and accepted as a man after God's own heart:

> *"And when He had removed him (Saul), He raised up unto them David to be their king; to whom also He gave testimony, and*

said, I have found David the [son] of Jesse, a man after mine own heart, which shall fulfill all my will."

(Acts 13:22)

King David's "Royal Secrets":

- He loved to worship God, privately and publicly.
- Whenever he stumbled, he poured out his repentance to God
- Although he knew he was called and anointed to be king, he did not move (to claim the throne) before his appointed time.

Esther

So you say you are not a person of means, and therefore unable to achieve great things? God's plans are not limited by our human abilities or resources. The story of Esther demonstrates that He works in mysterious ways to bring about His divine plan, requiring only our faith.

Long ago in the powerful kingdom of Persia, the king banished the royal queen from the palace and ordered a search for a new queen.

An orphaned Jewish girl named Hadassah lived in the kingdom with her older cousin Mordecai. She and other girls were brought to the king's house, where for twelve months they were prepared with beauty treatments of oils, perfumes, and purifications. She did not reveal that she was Jewish and adopted the name Esther. When the long awaited evening came for Esther to present herself to the king, he "loved Esther above all the women, and she obtained grace and favour in his sight more than all the virgins; so that he set the royal crown upon her head, and made her queen" (Esther 2:17).

So far, the story resembles a wonderful fairy tale. But the rags-to-riches story turns nightmarish. The king had an advisor named Haman, a wicked man who possessed the king's royal signet ring enabling him to validate any order that he commanded. Haman ordered a decree that all Jews be destroyed. Mordecai sent word to Esther, pleading with her to use her position as queen to go before the king and beg for the lives of the people. He asked this fully knowing that if anyone goes before the king without being summoned, the king could put him or her to death.

Imagine Esther's fear; her own life in one hand, the future of her people in the other! Esther ordered the Jews to fast for three days. She too humbled herself before the Lord God. She then risked her life by entering the inner court to see the king without invitation.

> *"… and so will I go in unto the king, which is not according to the law: and if I perish, I perish."*
>
> (Esther 4:16)

Finding favor in Esther, the king held out his golden scepter to her. (Whew!) The king told Esther to ask whatever she wanted and he would give it to her. She decided to wait until the timing of a strategically planned banquet in the king's honor to ask for the lives of her people. She exposed Haman's plan and in an ironic twist, Haman was put to death. Further, Mordecai was promoted and authorized to write a counter order for the deliverance of the Jews in the king's name!

God raised Esther from an orphan to royalty "for such a time as this" (Esther 4:14). *Queen Esther was just the right combination of gifts and talents for her assignment. So are you!*

Queen Esther's "Royal Secrets":

(A few of Esther's many qualities in addition to her outward beauty)

- *Teachable Spirit* – Humbly submitted to the advice and authority of her mentors. Willing to adapt to whatever process was required to be transformed into a vessel that was pleasing to the king.

- *Courage* – Willing to carry out her purpose on earth to save her people, even if it cost her own life.

- *Walked in wisdom* – Consecrated herself to gain the wisdom and strategy necessary to defeat the enemy's ploy plot. Understood that the timing of her assignment was critical to its success.

Royal Lessons

Joseph, David, and Esther; what can we learn from their stories?

As with Joseph, a slave and prisoner, you too have been "sent ahead" for an extraordinary purpose. Through whatever evil arises against you, never forget who you are, and know that God means it to work all for your good. Hear Joseph cheering you from the sidelines, "Hold to your dreams!" *May the Lord raise you up as ruler even in strange and ungodly places, to influence and guide a generation toward their destiny and speak increase into the land.*

As with David, a shepherd boy, may you rise to greatness in the presence of your enemies, being careful not to become corrupted by material things. And although you may make mistakes, repent of your human flaws, *may the Lord say of you, "I have found a man after mine own heart, which shall fulfill all my will."*

And *as with Esther*, an orphan in a foreign land, you were born into this dispensation with a divine assignment "for such a time as this." As His chosen one, may you carefully prepare yourself and intimately abide in His presence. There in His presence you will find courage. *May you find favor with the King who grants you access into high places, giving voice to the people of God, and influencing the laws of the land.*

> Step into the palace, into your wealthy place. You are God's royalty!

Step into the palace, into your wealthy place. You are God's royalty! Follow your journey through the pit and the prison. Overtake the lion and the bear. Outlive the giant, and outwit the wicked seated in high places. Through it all you will increase in wisdom, courage, and favor with God and man. *You will rise to royalty.*

May your kingdom be well. May your days be long and prosperous.

Reflections Of The Journey

- He has prepared "a place" for you!

- Your palace is a place where God not only blesses you, but makes you to be a blessing.

- Your kingdom is whatever God has given you dominion over or assigned you to oversee in the earth.

- The purpose of your kingdom is that you will be a demonstration of God's will being done "on earth as it is in heaven."

- If you want to inherit the kingdom, warfare is not optional.

- From Genesis to Revelation, God is speaking to us about taking our places as kings and priests in the Kingdom of God.

- God is over all kingdoms, but we carry His Kingdom within us, and we are called to reproduce it in the earth.

- Queen Esther was just the right combination of gifts and talents for her assignment. So are you!

- Step into the palace, into your wealthy place. You are God's royalty.

The Journey Continues . . .

Exercise

My Kingdom Assignment
(Are You Ready for Royalty?)

Your kingdom is wherever God has given you dominion or assigned you to oversee on earth.

Your Kingdom:

Identify your area of dominion (business, community, ministry, arts, etc.):

What group of people do you desire to aid, impact, or influence?

How well are you currently leading, inspiring or influencing in this area?

___ Need Improvement   ___ Good Progress ___ Great Impact

Your Assets:

What are your kingdom assets (talents, skills, successes, and strengths)?

What sets you above and apart from others with similar assets?

Your Royal Court:

Traditionally, the king ruled through the order of other nobles who officiated over smaller portions of the kingdom:

Who is managing warfare (praying and interceding) for you?

Who is generating/ overseeing finances for the vision?

Who is keeping watch for open doors, new ideas and opportunities?

Who is royal advisor?

Who are your heroes/ champions?

Perhaps it is time to reassess and re-establish what and who qualifies to share your time and intimacy.

Your Adversaries:

Every kingdom has enemies that threaten its existence. Do you know who your adversaries are?

What giant comes against you every time you try to excel in some area? What enemy has hindered the growth of your kingdom?

What have you conquered or overcome?

What steps will you take to prevent re-occurrence?

Your Strategies

What can you borrow from the stories of Joseph, David, or Esther to bring increase to your kingdom assignment?

Chapter 19
ARISE – It's Your Time

Pass Over This Jordan

You have come over hills and mountains. You have survived stormy seas. The mighty Jordan River is before you. Now that you have had a glimpse of the palace that awaits you on the other side, will you cross over? Will you take hold of your future, or be haunted by your past?

> *"Hear, O Israel: Thou art to pass over Jordan this day, to go in to possess nations greater and mightier than thyself, cities great and fenced up to heaven."*
>
> (Deut. 9:1)

At the end of their arduous journey, the Israelites entered the Promised Land by crossing the Jordan River. The actual crossing is the final step of the journey.

> You are standing at the edge of your miracle!

As they stood along the banks, all they saw was a mighty rushing river before them. They must have asked, "How can we ever cross over?" I'm sure you must be thinking the same. There is no bridge, no river boat. The only way to go across is by faith.

But be very aware of where you are. *Though disguised as a barrier, the river is actually the entrance to your promised land. You are standing at the edge of your miracle!*

Interestingly, the River Jordan was miraculously divided for the crossing over just like the Red Sea (Josh. 3:15-17). Why the same miracle as the Red Sea? The Red Sea represented coming out of Egypt's bondage. The Jordan River represented going in to the Promised Land. *By some miracle of God's hand, He brought you out of bondage, and by His hand He will bring you in to your promised land.*

How long have you been waiting to see the promises of God manifested in your life? For Israel, it had been forty years of wandering in the wilderness. Due to their doubt and unbelief, they were not permitted to enter the Promised Land at the first opportunity. Now, nearly forty years later, they had a second chance. And this time, they were ready to go forward.

Are you?

Go After It!

> *"And they commanded the people, saying, When ye see the ark of the covenant of the Lord your God, and the priests the Levites bearing it, then ye shall remove from your place, and go after it."*
>
> (Josh. 3:3)

Joshua instructed the people on how they must cross over—by following the Ark of the Covenant. The ark symbolized the presence and power of God with His people. The ark was the sign that God was leading them. When it's your time and you see that the hand of God is guiding you, don't delay. Your miracle is at hand. Move out from your place. Go after it! For as soon as the Levites carrying the ark put their feet into the water, the river immediately stopped flowing and stood up like a wall. Then all of Israel—millions of people—crossed over on dry ground. God was going before His people, and He opened the way. *Keep your eyes on God who is going before you and not on your circumstances. He has cleared your way to victory! Go after it!*

> *"...that ye may know the way by which you must go: for you have not passed this way heretofore."*
>
> (Josh. 3:4)

Joshua was very careful in saying, "for you have not passed this way before." Expect and prepare to pass over in ways that you have not seen before. We all have a great Jordan to cross. This is God's opportunity to demonstrate His power in your life.

Let it be.

Resurrection

I almost didn't make it to my promised land. At the river crossing, instead of excitement, I felt there was no life left in me. It seemed the journey had taken its toll. Think for a moment what that must be like, to feel lifeless, like being enclosed in a tomb. Darkness all around. No light can enter. The air is stale. No air moving around you. You can't breathe. You're constricted. Can't reach out, stretch out. You're walled in. Doom and despair on every side. Ever felt that way?

If only I had known how close I was to my breakthrough, I wouldn't have suffered such despair. I asked the Lord to die, twice. I had descended to the lowest part of my valley and simply did not see value to my existence. I didn't die physically, but I was buried in my tomb of hopelessness, and wrapped in grave clothes of gloom and despair. I was buried alive.

But thank God He took me by the hand:

> "Damsel, I say unto thee, arise."

"And He took the damsel by the hand, and said unto her, Talitha cumi; which is, being interpreted, Damsel, I say unto thee, arise."

(Mark 5:41)

When I was too depressed to get out of bed, instead of pushing snooze on the alarm clock, I pressed play on the tape recorder and let a beautiful song play over and over until I could muster up enough strength to face the day. Through the lyrics of the song Jesus was sweetly saying to me, "Arise."

He told me to ARISE!

Sometimes I would let it play all through the night so that I would hear it in my sleep instead of having nightmares. I could sense Him standing there looking after me. His eyes full of compassion. But it was up to me to choose life or death. I chose Him, the resurrection and the life (John 11:25).

As you are walking away from death, peeling off the grave clothes, He is coaxing you toward Him, toward the light.

A store owner I met spoke with a foreign accent. She introduced herself as Maureen, and then wrote it down for me saying, "It's English, you know." I asked if she knew what it meant and she smiled, putting her hand to her chest. "A secret place," is what I thought she said. "No, no. A sacred place. Like a place where you didn't expect something to happen, but God did. Like a miracle!"

"Oh, how beautiful!" I responded. Then I shared with her the meaning of my name.

I now believe my mother heard from God when naming me. Because I later learned that the meaning for Stacie is "resurrection" or "one who shall rise again." It also means "Rose of Jericho," derived from the Anastatica resurrection plant. The Anastatica is an interesting herbal bush found in arid regions, which curls up during storms and winter and looks like a weed or dead plant. Then with the first rain, it uncurls and comes back to life! That certainly has been my life's testimony. You can never underestimate the resilience of the human spirit.

Oh friend, how loved you are. Oh how valued you are. You're still here.

You may have plenty to feel sorry for, but the Lord is not going to give you a commentary on your life. He is simply going to say to you, "Arise." He is commanding you— Get Up!

There's nothing for you in that tomb. *There is no death, no defeat, no breakdown worth more than your breakthrough.* Be set free from your grave clothes. Prepare to ascend!

> Jesus rose again so that you could rise again.

The heart of Christianity is the resurrection. *Jesus rose again so that you could rise again.* He arose to give you hope.

Listen to the Sound

Listen…

Fruitful winds are blowing.

You can always tell when God is getting ready to move. It's like the quiet before the storm. All of nature pauses to listen. All the earth keeps silent before Him.

Ever notice how right before a hurricane or a tornado, the atmosphere changes, and the colors in the sky look strangely different? All birds and creeping things find a hiding place.

Silence. Stillness.

And then, a warm breeze. A rustling through the trees. The stirring of air, and you can just see the clouds begin to move by the rushing blowing of a great and mighty wind. And then it builds, and builds, and becomes a force no man can reckon with.

Now, even as the atmosphere around you is beginning to change, don't be alarmed; for it is necessary. You see, everything, even the air you breathe knows it needs to adapt and prepare for that awesome, new thing God is doing in your life. So don't be concerned with what you see, or what you feel, not even the force of those hurricane winds that are blowing in your life.

Just listen.

As the whisper builds and amplifies into a crescendo of all God's instruments, *everything and everyone that is instrumental in bringing you to your place of destiny is coming together in a beautiful symphony around your life.* Pure harmonies. Rich melodies. Raining down from the windows of Heaven!

Rise up and be enveloped in the breath of God.

Follow the sound that is ushering in your destiny.

Your New Beginning

It's time to try again.

You may not be as far down the road as you'd hoped to be, but you are turning a new corner. And there's a testimony written all over your face!

It's time for a new beginning. I know you've been down this path before, but it's different now. *You* are different now. The eyes of your understanding have been enlightened by the journey.

> *"And thou shalt remember all the way which the Lord thy God led thee these forty years in the wilderness, to humble thee, and to prove thee, to know what was in thine heart, whether thou wouldest keep His commandments, or no."*
>
> (Deut. 8:2)

The journey has made you stronger and wiser. *This time you will move in the Spirit.*

> The journey has made you stronger and wiser. This time you will move in the Spirit.

Let the past be the past. What do you do with it? Just lay it down. Behold all things are new. Along the banks of the river, go ahead and lay it down. Be no more drawn to it. Give no more thought to it. Not even a backward glance. Look on ahead; the glory of the Lord is leading you to your promised land.

You've endured many hardships but the fire did not burn you and the floods did not overtake you. You've sacrificed much. But all that you have given out comes back to you, so that you may give again. *Replenish your spirit. You cannot pour from an empty cup.*

Come and drink.

Because you were obedient in drinking from the bitter cup, taste now from a lush waterfall from which flows *perfect peace*.

Come and drink.

For the brook that was once dry now flows *an anointing of strength and restoration*. Drink it in.

Stagnant waters are now stirring. *"I will create for you an oasis,"* says the Lord. Be immersed.

There is a fountain. Plunge in beneath its flood and its *power to heal and to transform*.

Come and drink. You will taste. Ahh, and you will see that God is good, and that He is good to you.

Go now to a quiet place and let the Holy Spirit minister to you. He is waiting. In the stillness, you may not think that God is speaking. But *He is speaking directly into your spirit*, in a still, small voice. Breathe Him in.

Dancing within your spirit is a new song:

> *There's a seed of greatness planted within you – Awaken it.*
>
> *There's an appointed time for your moment – Take it.*
>
> *There's a glorious light of love shining on the path to your destiny – Embrace it.*
>
> *Embrace it until you learn to love it back.*

> Dancing within your spirit is a new song:

Receive all the light that is coming to you right now.

I'm talking to somebody that wants to rise up. I'm speaking to your destiny and I'm telling you that *it is still within reach*.

It's a new day!

I am your messenger sent forth to proclaim the words the Lord spoke to me in a dream as I was finishing this chapter: *"I hear even the whispers inside your heart. If you will be faithful over a few things, I will multiply the rest."*

He knows what you dream, what you long for. He hears what your heart whispers. God wants to bring forth what is inside of you. He wants to multiply it and greatly increase it.

> Live every ounce of what He placed inside of you!

Because you have journeyed, you now you have the assurance that your life is fulfilling a greater purpose. You are now keenly aware of your awesome value and purpose on this earth. Let nothing keep you from it. Walk out your destiny.

Live every ounce of what He placed inside of you!

It's Your Time!

Make one final notation at the chapter's end. This is your testimonial, your opportunity to give thanks and celebrate the wonderful work God is doing in your life. Just let it pour from your heart.

> Rise up, weary one. It's your time!

Think of what you've learned along the journey and how you've grown. Share the passion and excitement you have about your future.

Rise up, weary one. *It's your time!*

Imagine

Imagine what it will be like when the Lord calls His gifts home. Better known as the Day of Judgment, the final resurrection when every man will give an account of his works in the earth. How did you use His gifts, your precious gift of life? Who or what was edified because of your presence in the earth? Did you use your talents to promote your own agenda, promote the enemy's agenda, or build and uplift the kingdom of God?

Where will you stand when Almighty God asks, "What did you do with your dreams?" Will there be a sad silence in heaven, or will the trumpets sound in jubilation? "I gave you the gifts necessary to succeed in fulfilling your purpose in life," He will say. Will you be known throughout eternity as one who did not complete her destiny on earth? Or will Heaven rejoice at your coming and honor you as faithful and true to the call on your life?

Imagine.

What will He say of the one He "sent"?

Reflections Of The Journey

- It's time to try again.

- The River Jordan is the last great barrier before your promised land.

- Expect and prepare to pass over in ways that you have not seen before. Keep your eyes on God.

- The Lord is not going to give you a commentary on your life. He is simply going to say to you, "Arise."

- Do all that you were "sent" to do. Live every ounce of what's inside of you! Let Heaven rejoice!

Exercise

It's My Time! (A Testimonial)

*In your quest to know, and desire to do what
He "sent" you to do, please share:*

What did you learn about overcoming adversity on the journey to your destiny?

How do you see yourself differently?

What is the purpose of your gift(s)?

How will you "discover" your assignment on earth?

How will you use your gifts to walk in purpose, bring increase to God's Kingdom, and make a greater impact in the world today?

Celebrate the journey!

About The Author

Stacie Gaynor exudes the joy and passion of a woman who has dedicated her life to inspiring and uplifting others. As founder of *For Your Inspiration (FYI)*, she self-produced her first music CD entitled *"My Destiny"*. A compelling speaker, Stacie's *"Journey To My Destiny"* women's workshop series, based on her newly released book by the same title, equips others to walk in purpose, and empowers them to remove the barriers that block their destiny.

Stacie was recently honored as a Top 25 Women of Houston, receiving a U.S. Congressional award. Through her professional career with a Fortune 500 corporation, she invested more than twenty years working to improve Texas communities. She also served as company media spokesperson during several natural disasters. Her work in the community was recently featured on Houston's CBS and NBC affiliates. Her Anti-Bully Boot Camp presentation was live-streamed on KPRC TV, as she shared her personal trials and triumphs.

A gifted singer/songwriter, Stacie has performed on Houston's TBN & Daystar TV networks, and at some of Houston's most renowned venues. Her love for music and community intersected when her song "One Heart, One Hand, One House at a Time," was featured in the Habitat for Humanity International songbook with proceeds benefiting families in need of affordable housing worldwide.

Stacie holds a Bachelor of Science degree from the University of Pittsburgh. She is also a proud graduate of NAAWLI, a national non-profit women's leadership development organization who honored her as the 2009 NAAWLI Woman of the Year, as well as class spokesperson. She has also served the Texas Women's Empowerment Foundation (TWEF) in support of financial education for women. She was featured in "A More Excellent Way" women's magazine and was honored as a YMCA Minority Achiever.

For more information about
Journey To My Destiny workshops and retreats,
or to order additional copies of this book,
please visit us online at
www.journeytomydestiny.com.

www.ingramcontent.com/pod-product-compliance
Lightning Source LLC
Chambersburg PA
CBHW070139100426
42743CB00013B/2756